Y0-BZZ-406

**To Clients and Candidates of
Robert Half and Accountemps**

I'm happy to give you this copy of my book,
"The Robert Half Way to Get Hired in Today's
Job Market."

You might be interested to know it has been a
best seller, and was also a selection of the Book-
of-the-Month Club and The Fortune Book Club.

As an executive looking to hire, you'll find
information that will improve your interview and
selection procedures.

As a person looking for a new job, you'll find a
complete no-nonsense guide to the job finding
process.

So whatever your reason for reading the book,
I'm sure you'll find it useful.

Sincerely

Robert Half

accountemps

Rent an Expert ℠ ®

Accountants, Bookkeepers, Data Processors on a temporary basis—for a day. A week. A month or longer.

They're good enough to hire on a permanent basis (and many of them were).

Accountemps is part of the Robert Half owner operated organization, and is the world's largest specialized temporary service.

The Robert Half Way to Get Hired in Today's Job Market

Robert Half

BANTAM BOOKS
TORONTO · NEW YORK · LONDON · SYDNEY · AUCKLAND

THE ROBERT HALF WAY TO GET HIRED IN TODAY'S JOB MARKET

*A Bantam Book / published by arrangement with
Rawson, Wade Publishers Inc.*

PRINTING HISTORY

Rawson, Wade edition published November 1981

*A Selection of Book-of-the-Month Club (Fortune Book Club), February
1982 and American Circle (Bertelsmann) Book Club, June 1982.*

*Serialized in "Soundview Executive Book Summaries," April 1982;
"Jacksonville Journal," July 1982 and "Los Angeles Times Syndicate,"
July 1982.*

Bantam edition / May 1983

*The author and publishers gratefully acknowledge permission to
reprint the following material granted by the copyright proprietors:*

Form 103 © Copyright 1963, 1978—V. W. Eimicke Associates, Inc.;
Form 105 © Copyright 1963, 1977—V. W. Eimicke Associates, Inc.;
Form 115 © Copyright 1965, 1978—V. W. Eimicke Associates, Inc.
Form #23960 © Amsterdam Printing and Litho Corp.

*In life, very few worthwhile
things are done alone.*

I am fortunate to have had the help of many people in researching and compiling this book. My eighty managers in three countries, supported by key members of their staffs, assisted in producing a wealth of suggestions and comments. I have had expert editorial assistance from Barry Tarshis, Sanford Teller, A. Bernard Frechtman, James O. Wade, and John Boswell.

I appreciate the services of Burke Marketing Research, Inc. in compiling surveys the like of which have never been done before. And I'm grateful, of course, for the patience and understanding of my family during the two years of preparation for this book.

Contents

Preface

Knowing how to get a job is as important as knowing how to do a job.

I'm writing this book for two very simple reasons. I believe there are few things in life more important than finding a job that not only meets your financial needs and expectations but gives you psychological satisfaction as well. And I believe that there are very few people who understand how you go about finding such a job.

This book will tell you what more than thirty years in the personnel recruiting field has taught me about the techniques that work—and don't work—in job hunting. As you will quickly discover once you begin reading this book, it isn't necessarily the most "qualified" person who gets a particular job. More often than not, it's the person who has a special talent for convincing others that he or she *is*, in fact, the most qualified person for that job. Most of the candidates who are still in contention for a job in the final round of interviews are "qualified," and "capable," but only one person gets hired.

It could be you.

This book is not a collection of profound reflections on the philosophy of job hunting, nor is it filled with loose generalities. What I've tried to do here is to offer you sound, no-nonsense advice and practical, success-oriented tactics, based on my own experiences in the recruitment field, and based on the experiences of the managers in the more than eighty branch offices of the organization I head. The ideas that are at the core of this book represent the sum experience of more than 100,000 successful job placements.

I'm well aware, of course—and you should be, too—that there is no such thing as a "perfect" job, just as there is no such thing as the "perfect" candidate. But I've written this book with the notion that you should aim for a job that comes as close to perfection as possible—and give yourself every possible edge when the time comes to get hired for that job.

1

How Not to Get Hired

The person who does nothing has already made a mistake.

A few weeks ago I received a phone call from the niece of one of my closest friends. My friend's niece is in her late twenties and was a schoolteacher before she got married seven years ago. Now she is divorced and looking for a job. She'd started her job search, she told me, about six weeks ago, but didn't feel she was getting anywhere. She was discouraged and wanted to know if I could give her some advice.

I started out by asking her whether she was looking for a teaching job.

"No," she said. "I don't want to teach. I have a hard enough time with my own kids."

"Then what sort of job are you looking for?" I asked.

"I'm not really that particular," she said. "I just want a job that's interesting—something that will pay me enough to get by on."

I asked her where she had been doing most of her job looking, and she told me she was looking "where everybody looks—in the want ads." I asked her if she'd been to any personnel agencies, and she said she'd been to a couple but hadn't been impressed with the jobs they had suggested to her.

"How good is your résumé?" I asked.

"Résumé?" she said. "Well, I've been working on one, but I don't know what to say in it."

1

I'd heard enough. I told her, as diplomatically as I could, that I didn't think she was going about her job search in the most efficient way. I told her, for instance, that by not having a clear idea of what she was looking for, she was putting herself at an immediate disadvantage. I told her that while want ads are a good source for job leads, most job openings aren't advertised in the newspapers. You have to track down your own leads. I told her that a good résumé was an essential basic, and that at this point in her job search she should have her name listed with at least two or three good personnel agencies. In short, I told her that if she was serious about finding a good job, she was going to have to work at it much harder and much more systematically. "About how many hours a day," I asked her, "are you spending on your job search?"

"I don't know," she answered. "Whenever something comes up, I look into it." Then she added, rather defensively, "Looking for work isn't much fun, you know."

As if I needed to be told.

I have been in the business of filling jobs for people for more than thirty years, and the one word you will never hear me use in any description of job hunting is "fun."

Looking for a job is *not* fun. It's hard work—harder work, in fact, than most jobs. It's lonely. It's frustrating. It's discouraging. And it can be tough on your ego.

But as hard and as lonely and as ego-battering as job hunting usually is, it's something that nearly everybody past the age of consent has gone through at least once in life. And, like everything else, there is a right way of going about it, and a . . . well, not so right way. That is to say, there is a way of looking for work that *increases* your chances of finding a good job, and a way that not only *reduces* these chances, but makes you all the more discouraged and miserable in the process.

Now some people—perhaps you know a few—seem to be instinctively good at finding jobs. They may not be very good when it comes to *keeping* a job, or advancing their career once they're working, but they know how to get jobs, and they are never out of work for very long.

Most people though, are not particularly good at what might be described as jobmanship—the art of finding and getting a good job. Part of the reason, of course, is that the average person doesn't have much experience in looking for a job. But the big reason most people aren't very good at finding good jobs is that they go looking for work much like my friend's niece: haphazardly, hit or miss, with no sense of focus or direction, no clearly defined strategy. And this problem, incidentally, has nothing to do with basic intelligence, education, or present job level. I've worked with $100,000-a-year executives who hadn't the foggiest idea of what to do when they suddenly found themselves unemployed.

True, it's possible to get a good job today even if you're doing everything "wrong." Good jobs, after all, are opening up all the time, and somebody has to fill them. But the point is this: *the more you know about what works and doesn't work in job hunting, the better the chances that you'll be one of the persons to get the better job.*

Which brings us to this book.

The premise of *The Robert Half Way to Get Hired in Today's Job Market* is that looking for and finding a good job is an art that is independent of basic job qualifications and independent of whatever personal attributes may distinguish you from everybody else. I'm not suggesting here that qualifications and personal qualities *aren't* important and aren't going to go a long way toward determining the kind of job you ultimately get. But there's a big difference between having the "right" qualifications and the "right" personal qualities for a particular job and getting hired on the basis of them. The brutal and fundamental truth about job hunting is that "the most qualified person" is not necessarily the person who gets the job. It's *the person best able to convince the people doing the hiring that he or she is the right person for the job.* The art of finding a good job, in other words, consists not so much in *having* what you need, but in *using* what you have to the best advantage.

I can teach you this art; I can help you get hired for a job that's right for you. I can make this promise because I have been helping people get hired for nearly all of my adult life, and I understand the process for what it *is* and not for what it is sometimes painted to be in other job books. I know what employers are looking for when they interview job candidates, and I know how candidates routinely knock themselves out of the running without realizing how they've done it. I know the job search methods that produce results and those that simply spin your wheels. I know what I would do if I were looking for a job today and what I, in fact, did do many years ago when I had little trouble getting hired for a good job during a severe recession. And I know that my approach and methods would differ greatly from the approach and methods of most job seekers and, for that matter, from the approach and methods advocated by many of the job books currently on the market.

This is not a career guidance book. Except for emphasizing how important it is that you have a fairly clear idea of what you're looking for by way of a job, I'm not going to spend too much time helping you decide what you want to be when you grow up. What you want to do with your life and the kind of personal satisfaction you're expecting from your job are your affair. I can't tell you where to go, only the best way to get there.

Another thing you're not going to get too much of in this book is a lot of "keep a stiff upper lip" or "it's always darkest before the dawn" platitudinizing. To be sure, there is a psychological component to job seeking, and you need to come to grips with it, but I am not a psychologist—I am a specialist in getting people hired. So I am not going to tell you things about job hunting just to make you feel better. I am going to be as honest with you as I know how to be, and give you the same realistic advice I would give to a good friend. I have no ax to grind, no magic formulas or gimmicks guaranteed to get you hired by next Thursday—or even by Friday.

What you will get from this book is a lot of very solid, down-to-earth, success-oriented advice. You'll learn how to set up your own job search campaign, how to utilize your best source of job leads—personal contacts; and how to customize your approach to each job lead you follow up. You'll learn how to put together a résumé with "sell" in it, one that does more than simply list your background and qualifications. You'll learn how to generate job leads on your own. And you'll learn how to prepare for and do your best in job interviews—the moment of truth in virtually every job situation. You'll learn, too, how to organize your time and how to use it more efficiently than you may now be doing.

But don't expect *too* many shortcuts. Tough as it may be out there in the job market, you can be one of the winners— one of the people who gets a job he or she truly wants. Still, you're going to have to put forth plenty of effort. The Robert Half way can get you hired; but you're going to have to do the work.

Reflections on the Job Hunt

Nearly everybody has ideas and advice on what works and what doesn't work when you're looking for a job. The trouble with most of these ideas and this advice, though, is that they're not very useful. At best, the general advice you get from most people doesn't address itself to reality. At worst, it can waste a lot of time and effort.

Some "experts" advocate what might be called the "bold stroke" school of job hunting. The idea here is that you need some sort of gimmick in order to beat out the competition for a good job. You write your résumé in the form of a sonnet, or have it printed on fuchsia-colored paper. You park yourself on the doorstep of the company president until you get a personal hearing—make a pest of yourself, in other words. With a letter you send to the president of a company you want to work for, you include a photograph of yourself on top of an elephant. You go out of your way to be noticed.

True, in certain situations and in certain fields, you can be bolder in your approach. And certainly if everything else has failed, it doesn't hurt to try something unusual. But I would hardly recommend organizing an overall job search strategy around this sort of strategy.

Gimmicky approaches to job hunting are like trick plays in

football. Once in a while they work, but you can't devise an offense based on trick plays. The fundamentals of job hunting, as I see them, may lack glamour. They may seem tedious to you. But execute them well and you will succeed. The difference between successful job hunting and unsuccessful job hunting isn't so much the steps you take but how well you execute each of these steps: how strong a résumé you prepare, how compelling a story you tell in the letters you write, how enterprising you are in cultivating and expanding your contacts, how effective you are in the interview situation—in short, how well you market yourself as a job candidate. In other words, go the conservative route, but execute the fundamentals better than anybody else.

Just what are these fundamentals? Let's look at some of them.

In the first place, getting a job means getting somebody to hire you. This is an obvious point, but it's one that an astonishing number of job hunters never fully grasp. *Somebody—another human being—has to decide that you are, in fact, the right person for a particular job*. Whether you are the best person for the job isn't the issue: it's whether you are able to *convince* this person—the hiring authority—that you can handle the job better than everybody else being considered. Convincing this person amounts to making a $1 million sale, because if you are younger than fifty, chances are you're going to have earned at least $1 million before you retire.

But something has to happen even *before* this decision gets made. You have to stay in the running long enough to get into the interview situation. And even before this happens, you have to be aware that a job opening actually exists.

So, when we talk about the art of job hunting, we're talking basically about three things:

1. Tracking down job leads.
2. Responding effectively.
3. Winning the interview performance.

Let's take a closer look at each.

Tracking Down Job Leads

If it is true that getting a good job is often a matter of "being in the right place at the right time," it is equally true that being in many places vastly increases your chances of being in the "right" place. One of the things we're going to do in this book is to put you into as many places as possible.

"Places" are job leads—situations in which you have a chance at being hired. Some leads are obvious: ads in the classified section. Others you have to sniff out on your own. Personnel agencies and personnel recruiters are good sources of job leads, but the *best* source of job leads is the people you know: relatives, friends, colleagues. Indeed, virtually everybody you meet is a potential job lead source—*even the person who fired you*.

A big part of your education in job getting is learning how to utilize the contacts you already have. And, just as important, how to *expand*, or "pyramid," your list of contacts. Ideally, you are looking for contacts who can lead you directly to the person who makes the ultimate hiring decision, thereby reducing your chances of being eliminated. But any contact who can be a source of any promising job lead is a contact to be cultivated.

Responding Effectively (Getting to the Interview)

Two types of people should concern you once you begin tracking down a job lead: the people who have the power to say yes or no, and the people who have the power to say only no. File this in your mind and don't forget it: *Getting a job is largely a matter of avoiding the process of elimination that is basic to the hiring process.*

The reason most people don't get hired isn't that they don't fare well in the final job interviews. *It's that they never get that far to begin with.* Somewhere along the line—maybe the day their résumé arrives in the mail, maybe the day they go through the preliminary interview with somebody in personnel—they get dropped from consideration.

Unfortunately, the criteria that can get you dropped from consideration at any stage in the process may have nothing at all to do with your ability to handle the job. In some instance, the criteria are downright prejudicial. Depending on the situation, you could be dropped because you didn't go to Harvard or because you did go to Harvard; because your résumé was too long (in the mind of the personnel executive reviewing it) or too short; because you're a woman or because you're a man; because your résumé was clumsily written or because it looked to have been professionally prepared; because you're too short or too tall; too thin or too heavy; too talkative or too quiet; too ambitious or not ambitious enough; because you don't have enough experience or because you have too much experience. I've seen situations in which candidates were dropped from consideration because an interviewer simply didn't like the part of town they lived in.

It can get even more absurd. I had a client once say to me: "Don't send me anybody who is left-handed. Left-handed people are stupid." Another client gave me specific orders not to send him anybody who was from Brooklyn because, as he put it, "people from Brooklyn steal." I've had clients who were interested mainly in the candidate's birthdate, not because of how old the candidate was but because of the sign he or she was born under. I knew one executive who would only hire Capricorns—I often wondered what the office birthday parties were like in that company during December.

I mention all of this not to depress you but merely to impress upon you what is to be one of your guiding principles throughout this book: to be aware not only of what it's going to take to get you hired but of the factors that could knock you out of the running.

You can't control many of these factors—is it your fault that a personnel manager has a personal gripe against Aquarians, or about the college you attended? Still, you can protect yourself to some extent. How? By presenting yourself in so strong a light that *despite* arbitrary criteria, you stay in the running. Pulling this off involves what I call a "customized" approach to job hunting.

By "customized," I'm talking about an approach that

showcases those features about you that make you right for a particular job—right, that is, in the eyes of the people whose decisions determine whether you get the job or you don't get it. This doesn't mean telling lies or otherwise misrepresenting yourself. It doesn't mean playing a role you're not cut out to play. *What it means is highlighting those aspects of your background skills and personality that are relevant to each job you pursue.* It may mean having as many as four or five résumés all containing the same basic information, but each emphasizing a different aspect of your job experience. It means being able, on occasion, to adjust your personal style and manner in order to make a favorable impression on a personnel executive whose approval you need before you can be interviewed for the job you want.

Keep in mind that the goal of a "customized" approach to job hunting isn't so much to get the job but to get a *job offer*. And before you can think in terms of job offer, you have to get to the person who has the power to make that offer. Your route to this person may differ substantially from job lead to job lead, but your goal is always the same: *to get into the next interview situation*.

Winning the Interview Performance

You're sitting in the reception area of a company that has an opening for a job you definitely want. In a few moments you'll be called into an office for what could be one of the most important interviews of your life. How you handle yourself over the course of the next hour or so will determine whether you get the job or you don't get it.

If you're not nervous, you should be—at least mildly so. It's the bottom of the ninth in the seventh game of the World Series and you're up at the plate with two out, the bases loaded, and your team down by one run. You're either going to come through or you're not.

One of the basic goals of this book is to improve your job interview performance, and one of the first steps in gaining this improvement is recognizing that an interview is just that—a performance.

If you learn nothing else from this book, you will learn the best way to prepare for and to conduct yourself in this interview. You'll learn how to become an "overnight expert" on the company, and on the job you're after. You'll learn how to ask questions in a way that won't get you into trouble. You'll learn how to *answer* questions in a way that won't get you into trouble. You'll know ahead of time the kinds of questions you're going to get asked, and you'll know how to answer them, having rehearsed the answers beforehand. You'll learn how to "read" your interviewer, how to stay relaxed in the interview situation, how to deal with tactics meant to test your stress reactions.

Maybe you've messed up job interviews in the past, but that was yesterday. Remember, you need no special talent to score well in an interview. You simply have to know what to expect and how to respond—and you'll learn it in this book.

Clearing Up Some Misconceptions

One of the things you're going to be doing a lot of in your job search is making decisions. You will make these decisions largely on the basis of perceptions you bring to each situation. But your perceptions need to be based on facts, not myths. So before we do anything else, let's clear up some of the more common myths and misconceptions that frequently lead job hunters down blind alleys.

1. *It's a waste of time to apply for a job unless you have all the basic qualifications.*

Not at all. If your qualifications are reasonably close to the specifications of a particular job opening, and if you really want that job, and think you can do it, go after it! Qualifications, never forget, are only *one* of the things that determine whether or not you get hired. A survey conducted expressly for this book by Burke Marketing Research, Inc.—and I'll be referring to the results of this survey throughout the book— indicates strongly that the majority of people who do the hiring are more interested in you as a person than they are in your work background. True, the closer your qualifications meet the job specifications, the better your chances, but the gap between the two may not be as great as you think. A lot will depend upon how you present yourself.

2. *Once you've been fired, it's best to separate yourself from your former company as quickly as possible, the better to save yourself from unnecessary embarrassment.*

Certainly not—not if you can make some arrangements with your former company that can make life easier for you during your job search. Like holding on to your office, and maybe your secretary for a while, or keeping the company car for a few extra weeks. As a recently discharged employee, you have more leverage than you think. Many companies today recognize that having a lot of disgruntled employees around doesn't do them or the employee any good and so retain an outplacement service to help dismissed employees find another job. Don't let pride or self-consciousness keep you from getting benefits that could make life easier for you in your job search.

3. *It's silly to ask an employer who has fired you to give you a written reference.*

Again, not necessarily. It depends on why you were fired. Assuming that the reasons behind your dismissal weren't blatantly terrible, you can usually prevail upon your former employer to give you a favorable written reference. And while we're on the subject, resist the temptation—if you've been fired—to tell your boss once and for all what you really think of him or her. In a job search campaign, the enemies you don't have are as important as your allies.

4. *Executive recruiters aren't interested in you if you are unemployed.*

Executive recruiters, like all personnel services, are in the business of finding people for specific jobs. If you're the right person for the job, it doesn't matter whether you're currently working or not. True, most recruiters have only a limited number of jobs to fill, but this doesn't mean that you can't fill one of the openings. It doesn't cost much to send your résumé and a covering letter to recruiters—but concentrate on recruiters who specialize in your job or field.

5. *If you're interested in a particular company, the best person to approach is the head of personnel.*

In our Burke survey, personnel executives said almost unanimously that they rarely hire people, they only *screen* applicants for management. Probably the best person to approach—if you can get to that person—is a management-level person who works in the area you're interested in. The next best person is the company president, unless it's a giant corporation in which case you should contact the appropriate vice-president.

6. *Blind ads—i.e., ads that don't give the name of the company—are safe to answer if you're currently employed.*

Always approach blind ads with care. And never answer a blind ad if you are currently employed and want to keep your job search a secret from your employer. I've heard of situations in which companies place blind ads in order to find out which of their executives are looking elsewhere. And you have no guarantee that a recruiter who may get your résumé and letter won't turn around and approach your company with an offer to find your replacement, or that the letter won't be sent to a friend of your boss.

7. *The more unemployment there is, the tougher it is to find a job.*

Despite the obvious connection between unemployment figures and the number of people looking for work, the general unemployment figure doesn't necessarily mirror the difficulty you yourself can expect. For one thing, unemployment affects certain industries much more than others. Secondly, a substantial proportion of unemployed persons are very young or are people without special skills or training. Remember, too, that even during recessionary periods people are changing jobs. The annual turnover rate in corporations is somewhere around 25 percent per year on a national scale. And most of the time when a person leaves a job, the employer starts looking for a replacement. It could be you.

8. *Playing "hard to get" is a good strategy because it makes you a more desirable job candidate in the eyes of the interviewer.*

It's never smart to seem in *too* desperate need of a job—but you can easily go too far in the other direction, appearing so indifferent that your would-be employers are likely to think, "Why should we hire this person? He (she) doesn't even *want* the job." If you want a particular job badly, never create the impression that you *don't* want it. The lone exception to this rule is a situation in which you are being actively wooed by a company and playing hard to get might conceivably produce a more attractive offer. Otherwise, express the genuine enthusiasm you feel. This doesn't mean necessarily asking, after an interview, "Do I get the job?" It means coming out and telling the interviewer that the job is one you can handle and one you really want.

9. *Women don't stand as good a chance of getting a job in most white-collar fields today as men.*

Across the board, women today have as good a chance of being hired for most jobs as men, everything else being equal. We ran a study not long ago which showed that when at least one woman and one man were interviewed for the same accounting job in the $15,000 to $50,000 range, the woman got the job 72 percent of the time.

10. *You shouldn't waste your time going on interviews for jobs you don't really want.*

Getting a job offer isn't the only reason to go into a job interview. Impress the interviewer enough, and you might receive an offer for a job other than the one being offered. You might emerge from the interview with new job leads. At the very least, you'll gain some experience that might give you confidence to do better during an interview for a job you really want. I don't recommend that you make a career of seeking interviews simply for the sake of going, but, generally speaking, go on as many as you can.

11. *Never take the first job that's offered to you.*

The thing about the word "never" in job seeking is that it's never a good idea to use it. If you know ahead of time what you're looking for—that is to say, if you've done your homework—you should be able to tell whether to accept an offer or not, regardless of *when* that offer materializes.

12. *Taking a temporary job while you're looking reduces your chances of getting a good permanent job.*

Not true, depending, of course, on the sort of job it is and how it relates to the sort of job you're looking for. For one thing, a temporary job can help to ease financial pressure which, in turn, gives you more leverage, a stronger negotiating position. More important, temporary work frequently puts you into contact with people who may either want to hire you or may give you new leads. I've known situations in which companies have been so pleased with the performance of a "temporary" worker that they have "manufactured" a job for the person. The only thing to be careful about when you take a temporary job is that it doesn't drain too much of your focus and energy away from your full-time job—finding a permanent position.

13. *Once a company expresses interest in you, it's unethical to pursue other job possibilities.*

Not at all. A common pitfall in job searching is winding down prematurely. You get two or three situations that look "promising," and you figure that one of em is bound to come in. But too often the job situations don't pan out. You're forced to regroup and regain your momentum, which is always difficult to do once you've slipped out of the groove. The rule here is simple: never *assume* anything. There is no such thing as being "almost" hired. You either have a firm offer or you don't have it. If you don't have it, act as if your chances for it are remote. Pursue other leads.

14. *Whatever else you do in a job interview, try to "be yourself."*

"Be yourself" is sound advice in virtually everything you do, but part of effective job seeking is the ability to project different images of yourself, depending on the situation. I can remember years ago being fired from a public accounting job because the company told me they were looking for someone with a "heavier background." I thought about this and decided that the fact that I looked much younger than I actually was was working against me. So, I worked on projecting an image of maturity. Even though I only wore glasses for reading, I made it a point to wear glasses during my job interview, and I also made it a point to wear only very dark and very conservative suits for interviews. Once I locked up a job with one of the best CPA firms in the country, I stayed with this very conservative look and worked on developing certain mannerisms—slowing down my speech pattern, for instance—that would offset my youthful look. Mind you, during this entire period, I didn't necessarily *feel* older; but I recognized that my success was dependent upon my ability to convey a certain image, and I never interpreted conveying this image as a lie. I always knew I was a damn good accountant.

15. *Having a pleasant smile and being enthusiastic in a job interview isn't going to help your chances one way or another.*

Don't bet on it! Our survey shows that as many as 90 percent of personnel directors consider "basic enthusiasm" an important job qualification and although personnel managers don't often hire, they are in a position to eliminate you from consideration right at the beginning. In and of itself a nice smile and a pleasant manner might not get you the job, but they could be the factors that tilt the chances in your favor over somebody else, who wasn't enthusiastic and was stone-faced. Who would *you* hire under these circumstances?

Keeping on Top of Things

I said earlier I wasn't going to dwell too much on the psychological aspects of job hunting, but this doesn't mean I don't consider them important. On the contrary, your frame of mind throughout your search can't help but affect nearly everything you'll be doing. Certainly, it's going to color the way you come across in interviews.

Without belaboring what you may have already experienced first hand, let me say simply that looking for a job tests you in ways you've probably never been tested before. It puts pressure on almost every facet of your life: on your relationship with your spouse, with your children, and with your friends—particularly if a lot of your friends work for the company you've been forced to leave. It can interfere with your sex life, make it harder for you to enjoy your leisure pastimes. You may have trouble concentrating long enough to read a newspaper or to watch a movie. You'll probably be more short-tempered than you usually are. Fatigue may strike more frequently.

It's all to be expected. According to a "life events" stress table developed by a physician named Richard Rahe, loss of a job has more stress impact than the death of a close friend. In fact, out of more than fifty life events that Dr. Rahe maintains will produce stress in the average person, being out of a job ranks eighth.

Each of us, of course, reacts differently to stress, and some of us are undoubtedly better than others at resisting its effects. I'm hardly an expert on the subject, but I've always been interested in why some job seekers deal with the pressures much better than others. A lot of it, I'm sure, has to do with basic self-esteem and self-confidence—the inherent feeling that you're too good a man or woman to be out of a job for long. But don't ask me how you instill this in a person. I can still remember how devastated I was years ago when a woman who was interviewing me told me I wasn't worth the $15 a week (yes, $15 a week) I was asking. On the other hand, I've noticed that the people who deal with the pressures of job hunting best tend to operate differently from those who run into trouble keeping up their spirit. And it's on the basis of these observations that I offer the following list of suggestions designed to help you cope a little better. None of them is a panacea, and not all of them may have relevance to your situation, but keep them all in mind just the same. They could help.

1. *Establish a job search routine*. While you were working, you probably had a set routine, governed by the hours and the nature of your job. Being out of work, apart from everything else, completely disrupts this routine and the comfort you may have found in it. To counteract the tendency common among many job seekers to waste time (and then to feel guilty because of it), set up a schedule for yourself and follow it as faithfully as you would if you were still working and expected to show up at the job at the same time each day. Don't worry about "filling" this time. If you're conducting your job search in earnest, you'll have more than enough things to do to occupy your time.

2. *Don't keep your situation a secret*. There is only one truly valid reason for keeping the fact that you're looking for a job a secret, and that is if you still happen to be working and don't want to jeopardize your position. Otherwise, concealing the truth only increases the pressure you are already under and, worse, limits your job lead sources. Your most

fruitful sources of job leads are your friends and business associates. If they don't know you're out of work (or know it but don't want to offer help because you haven't asked for it), they can't do you much good.

3. *Put yourself on a budget but don't overreact*. You're undoubtedly going to have to set up some sort of a budget. It should be built around the money you have in reserve and the money you can expect from severance or unemployment, along with the amount of time you figure you'll be looking for work; but it shouldn't box you in so tightly that everybody in your family suffers unnecessarily. Don't be too quick to lop certain "luxuries" (beauty parlor appointments, for instance) off your expenditures list. Any expense that contributes to your appearance or your physical shape isn't a luxury when you're looking for work—it's a necessity.

4. *Keep a lot of irons in the fire*. At any given time in your job search, you should have not one but as many as a half dozen or so possibilities in the works. That way, if any one job you've been counting on falls through, you have other possibilities to fall back on. Keep in mind what I mentioned earlier about winding down too soon.

5. *Keep up your health—and your appearance*. Stress can often affect your ability to ward off sickness. It can cause you to gain weight you don't need or lose weight you can't really afford to lose. So be extra careful. Eat well-balanced meals. Take vitamins. Get at least some exercise every day, and try to spend at least a half hour a day, if not more, out of doors to keep a robust look on your complexion. Remember, nobody is going to hire you for a good job if you appear unhealthy.

6. *Don't withdraw from family and friends*. The people closest to you—your family members and your friends—can be enormously supportive, but you have to be open to their help. Don't be shy about asking friends for favors: you'll have plenty of time to show your appreciation. But don't

become a drudge or a bore. Looking for a job may be the most important thing in *your* life, but your friends and your family members have other interests, too. Fight the tendency to become self-absorbed and self-pitying.

7. *Take a temporary job.* Part time, ideally, so that you'll still have time to devote to your job search. Temporary work will not only ease the financial pressure on you; it will give some structure to your life and could well expose you to job leads that might result in good jobs. I can't tell you how many people who've used our Accountemps service (which employs people in temporary jobs) have eventually landed full-time jobs in one of the companies they worked with. Under certain situations I would even recommend taking on a volunteer job, especially if the job is something you enjoy and if it's possible to meet potential employers.

8. *Do something to improve yourself.* You're going to have a lot of empty time spaces to fill during your daily job search routine, so take advantage of them. Get well versed in a subject that's always interested you. Improve your vocabulary. *Use* the time productively, and the benefits can't help but make you more effective in the job search.

9. *Don't get your hopes up too high.* Probably the toughest thing to deal with when you're looking for work are job prospects that fall through just as everything looked as if it were going to come into place. To control this problem, resist the temptation to think of certain situations as being more promising than others. Take each step of each situation you move into one at a time. Don't get the champagne ready until the offer is signed and sealed. Above all, don't put too much stock in the "offers" you got when you were still working; chances are, they weren't genuine offers, anyway. The best way to keep your morale and spirit on the "up" side is to keep your hopes under wraps.

10. *Learn from your mistakes.* If you can learn something from the jobs you don't get, the disappointment won't be as

hard to take and you'll increase your chances for success the next time around. Don't waste time brooding about your bad luck. Always assume that there was something you could have done better to get you the offer. Try to figure out what it is, and don't make the same mistake the next time.

One final note. Under the best of conditions, being unemployed—as I've already mentioned and as millions of people today know firsthand—is an understandably discouraging state of affairs. And when there is very high unemployment, as there is today, the reality of the situation keeps bombarding you from all sides: in the newspapers, on television, and, in some cases, from friends, relatives and neighbors.

Practically speaking, of course, you can't *avoid* this reality. But allowing yourself to get caught up in all of this gloom and doom is not going to help you find a job and, if anything, is going to work against you. You start thinking to yourself, "What's the point of going through all of this trouble if there aren't any jobs out there?" and you stop doing the very things you need to be doing in order to find a job.

Mind you, I'm not suggesting that high unemployment doesn't compound the difficulty of finding a job. Neither am I suggesting that you delude yourself into thinking that the situation is better than it really is. Still and all, it's worth pointing out, I think, that, in certain not very obvious ways, high unemployment can work to your benefit—if you happen to be among the unemployed.

First of all, when there is high unemployment, people who are already working tend to become more security-minded than usual, so they stay put rather than look elsewhere. Consequently, in certain fields, the competition for qualified people is reduced. (I should add, too, that unemployment rates vary enormously from industry to industry and from specialty to specialty. Over the past few years, for instance, qualified electronic data personnel have had little problem at all finding jobs.)

Then, too, high unemployment—and the publicity that accompanies it—frequently leads people to do the very thing I'm urging you not to do: drop out of the job race. All of which means, that for those who stay *in* the race, the competition isn't quite as stiff.

Finally, in a period of high unemployment, your ego doesn't take as much punishment when your job inquiries don't produce the response you're looking for. "I'd feel a lot worse about being out of work," I heard a Chicago man say recently, "if it weren't for the fact that a lot of people I know are in the same boat."

I will grant you that it might be stretching a point to label the points I've just mentioned as "advantages." Then again, they do represent at least one small positive aspect of an otherwise bleak situation, so I wouldn't disregard them. For if I have learned nothing else over the past thirty years about job hunting as a process unto itself, I have learned that as corny and as obvious as it sounds, positive thinking *does* work and in a tight employment market, it's the *only* kind of thinking that works. I can't tell you *how* to keep up your morale and spirit—each of us has his own way of dealing with adversity— but I *can* tell you that the better you are able to handle the psychological difficulties of being out of work, the sooner you're likely to be back on the job.

II

Getting Started

If you prepare for every possible contingency,
you'll never get started.

Yesterday, you were looking for a job. Today, you're embarked on a job-search campaign. Every job-related action you take from here on should fall within the framework of this campaign. Everything you do will have purpose and logic behind it. It will be keyed to a strategy directed toward a specific target: getting hired.

Setting Up a Base of Operations

Your job-search campaign needs a campaign headquarters—a center of operations. It can be the office you worked in when you still had a job (assuming, that is, you've made arrangements to work there until you relocate). It can be a desk in the office of a friend or business associate. It can be a room or section of a room in your house or apartment.

You won't need much in the way of furnishings. A desk (or similar work area), a chair, a phone—those are the basics. A storage unit—a filing cabinet, perhaps—will be useful. So will a typewriter, if you know how to type.

Without investing too much money, make your work area as pleasant as possible. You want good lighting, for instance. If you're setting up shop in a basement area, spend a few hours and make the area around you as clean and as bright as possible. Keeping your morale up is going to be tough enough under normal circumstances. A dismal environment could make it tougher.

If you're working out of your home or apartment and the area you've set aside doesn't have a phone, have an extension installed, or get an extra long wire attached to your existing phone. The point is to have a phone within easy reach of your desk. An extension phone won't add all that much to your monthly bill and you can always get it taken away once you're working. In some situations—if, for instance, a spouse or roommate or children in the family use the phone frequently—consider having a separate phone installed specifically for job hunting. You'll incur some expense, but weigh the expense against the value of having a phone available to you whenever you want it, and against the tension that could arise when you want to make calls (or are expecting calls) and somebody in the house is on the phone. Generally, expenses related to changing jobs are tax deductible, but check this with either your tax advisor or the IRS.

If there isn't somebody—a secretary or spouse—who is competent and polite and has a pleasant voice to answer the phone for you when you're not at your headquarters, consider using either an answering service or a telephone answering machine. Relying on children (even teenagers) or domestic help to take your calls and collect your messages is risky. Heaven only knows how many jobs have been lost because a message was either not delivered or delivered incorrectly.

It's hard to say whether you're better off with an answering service or a phone machine. With an answering service, you have the advantage of an actual person taking care of the call, and you don't have to be actually at home to get your messages—assuming, that is, the phone machine you get doesn't have a remote device that lets you call in for messages. Another advantage of an answering service is that you pay as you go, on a monthly basis; there is no initial investment.

On the other hand, answering services with too many clients can be a little tardy sometimes in picking up the phone and have an annoying habit of putting the caller on hold. Then, too, if you want twenty-four-hour service, you'll have to pay extra. Neither of these things is a problem with an answering machine.

If you're buying a phone answering machine, there's no

need to get *every* feature available, but don't stint too much on the price, either: you want a machine that's reliable. Check the consumer magazines in your library for some comparative studies. Do some research among friends. Don't worry that having a machine might not make a good impression on a would-be employer. So many machines are in use today—I have one myself at home—that they've become an accepted part of business communication. When setting up the machine, have it answer on the first or second ring. Don't allow too long a gap between the end of your recorded message and the beep that signals the caller to leave his or her message.

The message itself should be brief and businesslike, but shouldn't sound too stiff. Here are a couple of suggestions:

"This is _____. Sorry I missed your call, but if you leave your name, number, and message after the beep, I'll get back to you just as soon as I can . . ."

"Hello, this is _____. I'm not here right now, but leave your name, number, and message, and I'll get back to you soon. Please wait for the beep before you start your message."

Some Added Basics

The big things you have to do throughout your job search will be easier for you if you do the little things in an organized manner. Here are some added items and suggestions that could help your campaign run more efficiently.

Personal stationery. All of your correspondence should go out on personalized stationery, the sole exception being your résumé. For most purposes, the standard 8½ × 11 inch will serve you well; but if you're in a high executive bracket, I recommend the monarch size (slightly smaller than standard) with your name engraved at the top (not raised lettering) in a simple, businesslike style. Just the name—no address or phone number. You include the address and phone number under your signature in each letter you write: it's a nice touch. Get a reasonably heavy bond, stick to basic colors (white, off-white, or ivory), and remember to order some plain sheets for the second page of your letters. The envelope should include your address (I like to see it on the flap), but if you live in a private house there is no need to put your name. A local quick copy center should be able to handle basic stationery needs, but for engraved stationery you may have to go to a stationery or department store. You may bridle at the price, but it's a worthwhile investment. Think of your stationery as being part of your appearance. It's often the first part of you that gets evaluated.

Secretarial service. Unless you're an excellent typist—and most of us aren't—make arrangements with a typist or a typing service. If you *do* type well, use a typewriter that has a clean, businesslike typeface: avoid the script or Roman-style typefaces. Your letters must not only be letter perfect, they have to look good as well. There are several ways you can handle secretarial service. You can use a commercial service, if one is convenient, but it's less expensive if you find somebody nearby who types part time. Check with friends whose secretaries might be interested in making some extra money.

Set up a system whereby you're feeding several letters to be typed at one time, as opposed to doing it on a hit-or-miss basis. (Simply having a person expecting letters could in itself be an inducement to write more.) Look into the possibility of having a secretary come into your headquarters for a few hours a week to take dictation. Or, experiment with dictating your letters into a tape recorder or over the phone. It all depends on the volume of your correspondence and the way you like to work. Hiring part-time secretarial help will cost you money at a time when you might not be able to afford it, but your time is worth money, too. If it takes you two hours to accomplish what a secretary could accomplish in fifteen minutes, you're wasting two hours.

A briefcase. A little thing, perhaps, but I know of many personnel executives who will judge you, in part, by the kind of briefcase you're carrying. If you don't own one already, buy a nice-looking briefcase or attaché case—something that doesn't look as if it came from a discount drugstore. Make it large enough to carry whatever you might normally want to take into a job interview, but not so large that it looks as if you're going away for a weekend trip. A good leather brief-case can be expensive, but it wears well. I advise against the ostentatious designer logo briefcases. I know more than a few executives who would drop you from consideration on the spot if you carried into an interview a briefcase on which you had spent an additional 50 percent simply for the sake of the name. By the same token, don't use the tattered and battered case you unearthed in your attic.

Directories. Having appropriate phone and address directories handy can save you an enormous amount of time and effort. If you live in a suburb but are concentrating your search in the city, get both a white pages and a yellow pages directory of that city, and make sure that both are *current*. Your local phone company will provide these directories to you free of charge, but it may take a while before the company gets them to you. To save time, pick them up yourself. Directories relating to your particular occupation or field should have a permanent place in your work area. If you haven't already discovered it, you can waste a ridiculous amount of time scrambling around looking for numbers or addresses.

A Filing System. You may not think so now, but once you get into the swing of your job search, you're going to begin to accumulate a ton of paperwork, and the better you're able to organize this material, the easier you will make it on yourself. For starters, get a 5×8 file box and cards to serve as a permanent file of job situations, leads, and influential business people. Each job situation you look into, whether it's a company or a specific job, should have its own card containing names, numbers, and other relevant information. You can use the cards to write yourself little reminders. Maybe the executive you spoke to this morning had a terrible cold: mark it down on the card. Two weeks from now when you call back, ask how he or she is feeling. A little thing, yes? But these are precisely the kinds of things that often make the biggest impressions.

A Logbook. I call it a ''logbook,'' but it's nothing more than a looseleaf notebook to be used as a daily operations log. Get into the habit of recording everything—everything—relating to your job search into this notebook: calls you've made, calls you want to make, names, numbers, reminders, ideas. Do it on a *daily* basis. At the end of each day, go through each listing, crossing out anything that is no longer important, keeping track of what has relevance for the future. To play it safe, keep on hand for at least a month or two daily log sheets you've gone over just in case there's a number or name you've recorded incorrectly.

A few other items that could make your job search run more smoothly:

Appointment calendar. Buy one that allows for hour-to-hour notations. It's a good idea to get one you can carry around in a briefcase or purse.

File folders. For sorting paperwork—letters, carbons, clippings, etc.—into easily located categories.

Bulletin board. Not essential but useful if you have room for it in your work area. A space 2 feet square should suffice. Use it to post notes and make reminders to yourself.

Stamps. Keep a supply of them on hand at all times. You have better things to do with your time than stand in line at the post office.

Other office supplies. A stapler and staples. Paper clips. A scissors or ruler (for cutting out clippings and ads). Scotch tape. Wastebasket.

Some of the suggestions above may strike you as simplistic and not really important in getting a good job. But I urge you to follow up on them. The pressures of job hunting, as I've said, are tough enough when all the little mechanical details run smoothly. The minute you begin losing numbers, misplacing letters, or running out of basics like stationery, stamps, and so on, you burden yourself with concerns that can only reduce your effectiveness. The small amount of time and effort (and, relatively speaking, expense) it takes to put together an efficient job search headquarters is minor compared to the time and money you'll waste along the way if you don't get organized properly. Most job seekers don't pay nearly enough attention to keeping track of, and following up on, job leads and situations. Setting up a system that pretty much forces you to do so gives you a big competitive edge.

Setting Your Sights

Once you've set up a basic organizational machinery, the next step in your job campaign (if you haven't already taken it) is to formulate job targets. Get a fix on what you're looking for. You can't get away with saying to yourself, as too many job seekers do, "I'll know whether I want the job when I hear what it's like." It's too passive an approach. You may *think* that by expressing a willingness to do "anything that's interesting," you're broadening your chances, demonstrating a flexibility that is going to impress your would-be employers. But it doesn't work this way.

This is what a friend who leads the personnel department of a major industrial corporation has to say about candidates, especially recent college graduates, who come into job interviews without a clear idea of what they're looking for:

"They act as if I'm a career counselor, which is not what I get paid to do. I don't mind answering some questions, but as soon as I get the idea that the person I'm interviewing isn't sure of what he or she is after, I immediately lose interest. I figure if people haven't taken the time before they come to see me to think about what they want to do, why should I take the time to solve their problems?"

A job that's "interesting." A job that's "challenging." A job that offers "opportunity," that will allow for "personal growth," or "personal expression." These are all admirable objectives. But unless you can tie these personal considerations into some fairly concrete goals, you run the risk of alienating a lot of would-be employers, regardless of your personal qualifications.

This isn't to say, of course, that you need to articulate the *exact* job you're looking for before you can start your job search in earnest. Indeed, as we'll see later, having too specific a job target can be almost as damaging to your chances as having no target at all. Nor is it necessary to have only *one* target in mind. Depending on who you are and what your background is, you could well devise a campaign made up of several different occupations and different fields—each of them, of course, requiring a slightly different approach.

How you go about formulating these targets is up to you. The most practical and realistic job target is one that relates closely to what you were or did in your previous job or what you're doing now. This is particularly true in the high salary brackets. It is almost axiomatic that the closer your job target is to your most recent job or to your past experience, in general the easier it is going to be for you to find a job you want, and the more money you can expect. (There are, of course, exceptions, the biggest being the possibility that you're in a field in which the job market is extremely limited.)

Beyond this basic criterion—that your job target be tied to your past job experience—the appropriateness of a job target has to do with your personal goals and attitudes: how much money you want, what kind of environment you're looking for, what specific features interest you in a job. Conceivably, these considerations may not be consistent with what you've done in the past, but this doesn't mean you have to disregard these considerations. Remember, you don't *have* to do anything you don't want to do in a job search. Just keep in mind that as important as these personal objectives are to you, they do not necessarily enhance your attractiveness as a job candidate. The person who hires you is obviously concerned about your involvement and commitment, but is more concerned whether you are the right person for the job.

Constructing Job Targets

A marketing position in the food industry that offers a salary of at least $25,000 a year—preferably with a small but up-and-coming company.

An editing position on a consumer magazine that pays at least $20,000 and carries with it the chance to become a managing editor within a few years.

An account executive position with an advertising agency that works a great deal in television, with a starting salary of *at least $30,000 a year. Preferably a job that doesn't involve much travel.*

A controllership position at around $45,000 in a manufacturing company.

These are four job targets that meet the criteria I like to set for job targets in general. They are specific but not overly so. Each represents a mixture of requirements and preferences.

Each job target you formulate should represent a similar mixture: a mixture of what you *need* and what you would *like* to have. The degree to which this target is shaded in one direction or the other will, of course, depend on you and on the marketplace. The general guideline is this: the stronger your background and qualifications, and the more favorable the job marketplace, the more you can allow the luxury of incorporating preferences—as opposed to needs—into your targets.

But there's a personal dimension here that doesn't lend itself to generalizations: your current employment status. Depending upon how long you've been out of work or how anxious you are to leave a job you now have, the relative importance of preferences and needs to the targets you set could vary. Job targets, in other words, are not fixed entities. A month ago your salary "requirement" may have been $30,000. If you've been running into a stone wall, you have to switch that "requirement" to a "preference" and set a slightly lower "requirement." Reexamining from time to time the job targets you set is a basic ingredient in a well-organized job search campaign. You should be doing it at least once a month.

Deciding What's Important

What is a requirement for you may be a preference for me, and vice versa. You may not care about where you have to move in order to get a particular job. Because of family considerations, I may be adamant about staying in the city where I now live.

In helping candidates clarify job targets, I've always found it useful to classify job target criteria into two basic categories: primary and secondary. (There's no reason you can't really add two or three more categories if needed.) Into the primary category go those job features that you are either unwilling or unable, for some reason, to compromise on. Money, for instance, is obviously a primary consideration: any job you take should at least pay enough to meet your basic living expenses. (There is one exception here: sometimes in a job campaign, it may be prudent to take a job that doesn't meet your salary requirements *for now* but positions you for *another* job with hose requirements.)

Commuting time, on the other hand, is usually a secondary consideration. It would be nice to have a relatively easy commute, but most people (though not all) will put up with commuting inconvenience if the job is attrac .ve enough.

Opportunity for advancement could be either primary or secondary, depending upon your situation. If you are a person whose spouse is already earning a good living and if you are looking for a job mainly because you'd like to get involved as opposed to establishing a career, advancement isn't as important to you as it may be for somebody anxious to move up the corporate ladder. The same can be said for the job environment. If it is important that you work in an easygoing environment with people you like, then job environment becomes a primary consideration. If these things *aren't* terribly important to you, environment becomes a secondary consideration.

The point here is that what is primary and what is secondary is highly subjective. Make sure when you're setting up categories that you separate primary from secondary considerations on the criteria that relate to *your* situation.

Breaking It Down

I've had candidates insist they didn't care *who* they worked for or in what industry—they simply wanted a data-processing job that would pay them at least $35,000. I've also had candidates armed with a list of three or four companies, saying that these were the *only* companies they would consider working for. I've received similar lists of companies a person didn't want to work for. I can remember one executive whose target specifications were so specific they even included the make of company car he wanted to drive. I was tempted in that situation to ask the man if he had any preference with respect to upholstery, but I held my tongue.

Only *you* can decide which job features—title, money, responsibility, location, company, field, etc.—are of primary importance and which are of secondary importance. But here are some principles to bear in mind when you're making these decisions.

1. *The occupation*. Your occupation, of course, is what you do—or have been trained to do—for a living. It's your specialty, your career. You're a salesperson, a teacher, an engineer, an accountant, a chemist, a computer programmer, a writer, a camera operator, a chef, and so on. Even though you are out of work, you still have an occupation. But the fact that you have a particular job may not mean that this job is your occupation. The waiter who took your order the last time you went out to dinner might describe his occupation as "acting." The man who cleared the leaves from your yard last month may be a teacher temporarily out of work.

If you are the typical job seeker, you are probably looking for a job in your particular occupation, which is to say that occupation is a *primary* consideration. If it isn't a primary consideration to you, it is for the person who is thinking of hiring you. If I have an accounting position open, I'm looking for an accountant, not an insurance salesperson who wants to become an accountant. If I have a position open for an insurance salesperson, I'm looking primarily for someone whose occupation is selling insurance, not an accountant who wants to sell insurance. True, I may be so impressed with this accountant who wants to get into insurance sales that I choose this individual over other candidates. But I have to be *very* impressed.

2. *Money*. Money is almost always a primary consideration. If it isn't, you're very rich, have a rich spouse, or have figured out a way to make a decent life for yourself without

money, in which case you don't need this book. But it isn't only the *minimum* amount of money you'll settle for that's the issue. I know of some candidates who actually set a *ceiling* on what they want. Years ago, a man told me he didn't want to earn more than $15,000 a year.

"But with your qualifications," I told him, "you could probably get $20,000 or more."

"I don't care," he said. "I can get along with $15,000. If I earned more, I'd risk losing the job if the company goes through a tough period."

One important reason for taking the money part of the job seriously is that if you don't, you may scare off a would-be employer. Say to a would-be employer, "Money isn't important to me," and the employer will immediately think, "Here is somebody I'm not going to be able to control." Goodbye, job.

Better to say something like, "Starting salary isn't as important to me as the future," and go on to express your confidence that once the company has had a chance to evaluate your performance the salary will be adjusted. In the event the job is offered you and the salary is *less* than your present earnings, you can always hedge and say that when you said salary wasn't as "important as the future," you never expected the offer to be *less* than your current salary.

The lesson: *Even if money doesn't really mean that much to you, and even if you don't need the money to live on, keep this information to yourself*. Otherwise, your job target should include a basic salary figure—what you need to cover living expenses and then some. (In the next chapter, we'll get to how you can best determine your asking price.)

3. *The field*. "Field" is a tricky concept, and far too many people use it interchangeably with occupation. Try to keep the two separate. Writing is an occupation; advertising is a field. Engineering is an occupation; electronics is a field. Selling is an occupation; insurance is a field.

Generally speaking, it's not as important to incorporate a specific field into a job target as it is to be able to pinpoint a specific occupation and the salary you're expecting. But it certainly gives more direction to your job search to narrow your target down to a single field, or no more than two or three fields. In some situations, a company will be more interested in your field of experience than in your general occupational experience, and it's important in these instances that you are able to articulate your reasons for being drawn to a field and the qualifications that make you right for it. Recently, I heard of an advertising salesman who landed a very good job as the ad sales director on a food and wine magazine. He had no experience with this kind of a magazine, but he was a good advertising man and, more important, his hobby was gourmet cooking. He knew the field.

Some fields, by virtue of their image and their glamour, are inherently more attractive than others, but this does not necessarily mean that the jobs themselves are any better. In fact, the opposite often holds true. Because the demand is greater, companies in certain glamour fields, such as entertainment, publishing, and advertising, can get away with offering lower salaries than you would accept in a different field.

It's only normal, of course, to be attracted to a field because of its image. And it's true that the more low-keyed and conservative a field is—banking, for instance—the more likely the people you work with are going to be low-keyed and conservative. The danger, though, is getting so caught up in the glamour of a field that you're blind to good opportunities in other fields, blind to the limitations you place yourself under by taking a job simply because it's in the field you want. I'm sure you've heard the joke about the man whose job at the circus was to follow the elephant around the ring and pick up the leavings with a broom and shovel. He wouldn't dream of looking for another job because it would mean "quitting show business." Well, I know a number of people in similar situations, one of them a woman who does administrative work with a major radio station in New York and admits the place has the atmosphere of a prison camp. "I'm really miserable there," she says. "But I love to tell peopie I work there because it sounds exciting." So does show business.

Here are a few random thoughts on fields to file away in the back of your mind:

• The longer you stay in a particular field, the more likely you will be typecast as one who is part of that field. You're no longer thought of as an accountant but a "real estate accountant"; you're no longer an engineer, but a "road construction engineer." There are both advantages and disadvantages to this. One advantage is that there are relatively few people like yourself, which means you can sometimes demand—and get—more money. One disadvantage is that you sacrifice flexibility: someone might interpret the fact that you've been so long in a particular field as meaning you can't do anything else.

• The more glamorous the field, the more competition you'll run into for jobs and the lower the entry-level and middle-level salaries will be.

• No field has a monopoly on "good jobs" or is completely without "bad jobs."

• I know unconventional people who are happily employed in very conservative fields, like insurance. I know conservative people who are happily employed in offbeat fields, like the recording industry. What does this mean? It's the job, not the field, that determines job satisfaction.

• It's easier, in general, to change fields than to change careers. In fact, you can use a change of fields as a vehicle for changing careers. A lawyer I know began with a typical law firm but decided he wanted to go into the entertainment business. He took a job as a lawyer for a large entertainment company, but within two years had worked himself into the business and production side of the company. Without that interim, transitional move, he could not have gotten the same kind of job.

4. *The company.* There are big companies, little companies, family-owned companies, multi-national companies, companies that have an almost paternalistic regard for their employees, companies that have no regard for their employees, companies that are known for offering quick advancement but

not much security, and companies that are big on security but slow when it comes to advancement.

It's probably a good idea to have as part of your job target a general sense of the kind of company you want to work for, but don't set your sights on certain companies—or make up your mind to avoid certain companies—simply because they have a reputation you may not like. First of all, what you've heard about a company may not apply to the division you'll be working with and, for that matter, may not even be true. Secondly, you'll have plenty of chances once you begin interviewing to see for yourself whether the environment is one you would feel comfortable in. Chances are, if you're wrong for the environment, the company will recognize this sooner than you do.

In any event, the following list will give you a sense of some of the options open to you. These are some of the different kinds of companies you might end up working for:

• A large, national or multi-national corporation in which career advancement may mean being willing to relocate from time to time.

• A smaller, locally headquartered company in which relocation is unlikely.

• High involvement company—one in which it's taken for granted that you'll arrive early and stay late.

• Low involvement—in which work is pretty much a 9 to 5 affair.

• A company with a highly competitive atmosphere that offers speedy advancement.

• A less competitive company where you're unlikely to get fired as long as you do a reasonably good job.

• A company known for its social consciousness.

• A company in the midst of rapid expansion.

• A company with a less dramatic growth pattern but one known for its consistency and stability.

• A company that is losing money, which offers you the chance to be a hero.

5. *The position.* The position is the specific job being offered: its title, its salary, its duties and responsibilities, and all the intangible elements that relate to the amount of satisfaction you derive from it.

You're making a mistake if you build your job strategy around too specific a job position target. First of all, the same title may mean different types of jobs in different companies. You decide you want to become the director of public relations for a hotel. Such an opening may exist, but because some hotel companies lump public relations with marketing, it may be described as director of marketing. Also, whatever you do, don't get caught up in the beginning of your job search with all the various cosmetic aspects of a job—the kind of office you're going to have, the number of people who will report to you, the flexibility you'll have with your hours. Rid your mind, in other words, of the image of the "ideal job." For all intents and purposes, it doesn't exist. Get a job that approximates this ideal, and once you're in the job, *then* make changes that will make it more suitable for you.

Job Target: Summing Up

Having job targets gives your campaign a structure and direction it wouldn't otherwise have. Formulate them on the basis of what you *need* and what you would *like* in a job, and don't confuse the two. Start with your occupation (or occupations), add a basic salary requirement, pick the field or two you'd like to be in, and you've got enough to work with. Stay flexible!

How Long Before You Get Hired?

As you can well appreciate, it's difficult to estimate how long it is going to take you to find the job you want. It depends on many different things, not the least of which is how selective you intend to be.

Even so, part of setting up a job search campaign is setting up some sort of projected time frame. Years ago I developed a system that works as well as any I've ever seen.

You begin by taking your present or last salary, including bonus and fringes, knocking off the last three digits, and dividing by 2. The figure you come up with is your base number of weeks. So, if you were making $20,000 in your last job, your calculations would produce a base number of 10, or 10 weeks. A starting figure of $40,000 would produce a base number of 20, or 20 weeks.

Another way of figuring this estimate is 1 week for every $2,000 in salary you were making before.

Once you have a base figure, you're ready to figure into your estimate some of the following individual considerations:

Your competitive qualifications. If they are high, deduct 20 percent from the base figure (for 20-week base figure, you'd now have 16 weeks, etc.). If they are low, add 50 percent (the 20 now becomes 30). If they're average, do nothing.

The "exposure" factor. If you intend, for whatever reason, to keep your job hunt a secret—which is to say, you'll tell almost no one that you're looking, multiply by 2.

Personal characteristics. If your appearance, personality, and communications skills are excellent, deduct 20 percent off the new figure. If they're poor, add 50 percent. If average, do nothing.

Your specific requirements (location, size of company, etc.). If these are highly specific, add 20 percent. If they're not critical, deduct 20 percent. If average, do nothing.

Salary demands. If you're looking for an increase of 20 percent or more, add 50 percent to the figure. If you're willing to take a 10 percent decrease in salary, deduct 20 percent. Otherwise, do nothing. Note: these figures relate to unemployed job seekers. If you're working, figure a 25 percent increase in the base figure when you're looking for a 20 percent salary increase. A 5 percent deduction in the base week figure if you're willing to take a 20 percent decrease in salary.

If your final calculation is *less* than your base number of weeks, insert the base. Otherwise, the final figure you get

JOB SEARCH TIME—A GUIDE

Your present or last annual salary (with bonus)   ——

Your base of weeks (omit last three digits of salary above and divide by 2)   ——

Competitive qualifications:
     High—deduct 20%   ——

     Low—add 50%   ——

Not willing to take risk
     Multiply by 2   ——

Personal characteristics
     Excellent—deduct 20%   ——

     Poor—add 50%   ——

Requirements
     Critical—add 20%   ——

     Not critical—deduct 20%   ——

Salary demands (if unemployed)
     Increase of 20% or more—add 50%   ——

     Decrease of 10% or more—deduct 20%   ——

Salary demands (if employed)
     Increase of 20% or more—add 25%   ——

     Decrease of 25% or more—deduct 25%   ——

Final job search time in weeks   ——

NOTE: If this figure is lower than base number at top, use original number. Also: don't attempt to use this guide if you intend to change careers. Depending on the circumstances, the change may be unconscionably long, even if you're willing to make salary sacrifices.

represents the number of weeks you should figure on your job search taking.

The chart on page 41 will help you to make your own calculations.

If You're Still Employed . . .

Looking for work while you still have a full-time job injects obvious complications into the job hunt process. Still, the psychological cushion it gives you is far too important an advantage to surrender. Even if you're not pleased with the progress you are making in your job search, and even if you're unhappy in your current job, don't be in a hurry to jump.

Two problems arise when you look for work while still working. One is purely logistical: finding the time and energy to devote to the job hunt when the major share of your time and effort is going into your job. The other is confidentiality: keeping your job plans a secret.

Don't underestimate the difficulty of keeping your job plans secret, and don't underestimate the consequences of being found out. Occasionally, if your employers get wind of the fact that you're looking elsewhere, they may make an offer that could induce you to stay. Our studies show, however, that most employees who accept a counter offer from their current company usually leave within a year, anyway. More money and added perks, apparently, don't defuse the basic ingredients of discontent. Usually, as soon as your company suspects that you're getting ready to leave, you can consider yourself as good as fired—whether you find a new job or not.

How ethical is it to look for one job when you're still working for somebody else? It's hard to say. If one of the companies you're talking to is a direct competitor to your present company, and if in your current job you're becoming privy to information that could aid the competition, ethics and laws relating to trade secrets become an issue. Which explains why some contracts forbid an executive from taking another job with a rival company until a certain amount of time has elapsed.

Then again, no one can condemn you for wanting to advance your career. In the end, the ethics involved in this situation are a matter of your own sense of propriety.

But ethics apart, watch your step. If I were working at one job and looking elsewhere, I wouldn't tell *anybody* in the company—not even my secretary, although I recognize that this isn't easy. Loyal as my secretary may be to me, who is to say that a secretary might not spill the beans inadvertently?

Don't tell even your closest friend in the company what you're up to. I heard recently of an advertising executive who told a man he thought to be a very close friend that he was looking around for another job, only to discover within a few days that his "friend" was making a pitch for his own position. I need hardly add that the two are no longer friends.

Be careful, too, that you don't give yourself away, which is easier to do than you may think. Seasoned managers have a sixth sense that tells them when an employee is looking around for another job. If you don't want to draw attention to yourself, give heed to the following points:

1. Don't begin taking noticeably longer lunch hours than usual and be careful about being absent from work too frequently. Both changes in your normal pattern are red flags that signal you're out getting job interviews.

2. Keep personal phone calls to a minimum. The surest way to arouse the suspicion of a secretary is to take a lot of calls you'd rather the secretary didn't know about.

3. Maintain your normal level of communication with management. Staying out of sight is an almost certain tip-off that you're planning a move.

4. Don't begin coming to work dressed noticeably better than usual. The immediate question your appearance will arouse is: "Why does he/she look so good today?" A job interview will loom as a possible answer.

5. Don't begin clearing your desk of personal effects.

6. Don't make a noticeable change in your vacation pattern. Managers know that employees who intend to leave frequently take a vacation just before announcing their decision.

7. Don't be less aggressive in the office than you usually are. Recently I heard of an advertising executive who thought he was being super-careful about his job search, but was nonetheless called aside by his boss, who asked why he was thinking of leaving.

"What makes you think I'm thinking of leaving?" he countered.

"Because," the boss said, "you're being too nice. We haven't had a good argument in a month!"

Tempting though it is, don't use your current office as any sort of job headquarters. And even if you have a little bit of freedom in your job, don't be too eager to set up interviews during normal working hours. Your current employers may not find out but your would-be employers might question the dedication of a person who was out on a job interview while still on company time. If they know you're working, the company you're talking to about a job will usually make arrangements to see you either before or after normal working hours. And letting your would-be employers know that, dissatisfaction apart, you still feel as if you owe your current employer an honest day's work isn't going to hurt you one bit.

III

Getting to Know the "Product"

*Nobody wants to fail, but some people try harder
than others.*

Imagine for a moment that you've just taken a job as an encyclopedia salesperson and you've made up your mind to become the top salesperson in the company. What would you do?

For starters, you'd probably acquaint yourself with the chief selling features of your particular brand of encyclopedia—what makes them better than the competition. You'd work on a sales approach that would present these features in as persuasive a way as possible, which means getting your would-be customers to see how this encyclopedia would benefit them. That's basic salesmanship. No matter how good the product is, you still have to appeal to the customer's need. You have to give the customer a compelling reason to buy.

You're on your way. Well, almost. Before you can launch into your sales pitch, you need to get past the front door. You have to spruce up your appearance. And you need an opening line to overcome the resistance you can normally expect with every doorbell you ring.

You will also have to learn—and this is something only experience can teach you—how to orchestrate your sales approach: when to talk and when to listen, when to ask questions and when to answer questions, when to talk about the product and when to talk about the customer (or the weather), when to move in and when to ease off. With experience, you'll get better and better at it.

You see what I'm driving at, don't you? You're right. Looking for a job isn't all that much different from selling encyclopedias (or, for that matter, selling anything), the chief difference being that the product in this case is *you*. Otherwise, the general approach is pretty much the same. You have to figure out what makes you "saleable," special. You have to develop the most persuasive way of communicating what makes you special, appealing to the *needs* of the would-be employer. You need a strategy designed to get you by the front door—past the office of personnel and into the office with the ultimate hiring authority. Finally, you need to become skilled in the personal give and take of job interviews.

In this chapter, we'll look carefully at the first aspect of this process: getting to know yourself.

What Do You Have to Offer?

There's an old joke about a man who brings a talking dog into the office of a booking agent. The booking agent is one of these gruff, jaded souls who has had his fill of talking dog acts and doesn't want to be bothered. But the dog trainer begs for an audition. "Look at this," he says to the agent. "Fido? What's on top of a house."

"Roof, roof," the dog yaps.

The agent shakes his head in frustration and once again asks the man to leave the office.

"Wait a minute," the trainer says. "Fido, name a candy bar. Baby . . ."

"Roof, roof," the dog yaps again.

Now the agent is really losing his cool. He stands up and orders the trainer to collect his dog and leave at once.

"But wait until you see this," the trainer begs. "Fido? Who was the greatest home-run hitter who ever lived. Babe . . ."

"Roof, roof," the dog replied.

The agent blows his stack. He sweeps around his desk, snatches the trainer by the shoulders, opens the door to the hall, and hurls the trainer out. Then he comes back and kicks the dog out after him.

Now the trainer and the dog are in the hall with the door slammed shut. The dog looks at his owner, shakes his head, and says in a clear voice: "I guess I should have said Hank Aaron, eh, boss?"

The moral to this little story is simple enough, yet it is one aspect of job hunting that most candidates don't appreciate nearly enough. If you are the trainer of a talking dog, it's up to you to get that point across to the people you need to impress as quickly and as emphatically as possible. You don't keep your assets a secret. It's not up to the company you approach to "discover" the facets about you that make you the best person for a job. *You* have to communicate these qualities. Not always directly, mind you. Sometimes you have to be subtle. But you must know that the qualities are there and how to direct your presentation of those qualities to the person who may hire you.

Developing the ability to sell yourself effectively has a dual dimension. First, you analyze all those aspects of yourself that contribute to your attractiveness as a job candidate. Then you relate these assets to the needs of the marketplace. You must have a clear idea of where your strengths lie—and where your weaknesses lie. You need respect for certain features about yourself that you may not consider great assets. Too many candidates downplay the importance of simple virtues, like being honest and trustworthy and dependable, or having a pleasant smile. Too many job candidates have never thought to count as a solid asset the fact that they are personable, likeable, and easy to be with. Yet our surveys show that personnel executives and top management executives place great importance on these traits. Being honest or trustworthy or dependable or likeable may not, on their own, get you hired, but you can be quickly eliminated from consideration if you appear weak in any of these categories. And you can sometime get the nod over somebody else if you come up particularly strong in any of these areas. I myself, when faced with a decision between two or three people who all seemed equally qualified, have frequently gone with one person for no other reason but that he or she struck me as being the more dependable. In retrospect, it dawns on me that I made this decision on the basis of how the candidate *presented himself or herself to me*. I remember one executive in particular who came right out and said: "I don't know whether you've made up your mind or not about me, but I'll tell you one thing. If I get this job, I'm going to be here every day giving it 110 percent. I won't let you down." The man was a good salesman. I bought the "product" and he didn't let me down.

What the Marketplace Is Looking For

Everybody stresses the importance of developing early on in your job search a solid sense of what you have to offer a potential employer. I have no quarrel with this advice; but it's important that you keep in mind, as you're analyzing yourself, what the *marketplace* is looking for. It isn't enough to draw up a list of your special qualifications and assets. There's a further step: translating these qualifications and assets into a form that has relevance to a potential employer.

Some examples: You think of yourself as industrious. Fine, but present yourself as someone who will "stay at the desk until midnight if that's what it takes to finish a project." You think of yourself as an organized person. Fine, again. Present yourself as somebody who can "keep things on track no matter how hectic the going gets." Know what you can offer and what you can do. Present these qualities in the context of what you think your would-be employers need. That's the basic principle at work here. It isn't so much what you have going for you that will get you hired; it's your ability to make your would-be employer believe that what you have is what he or she needs.

It Starts with Credentials

The first thing most companies want to know about you is what you've *already* accomplished. Your track record. Your credentials. In most job situations, for better or worse, nothing will have more bearing on whether or not you get hired.

It's easy to figure out why this has to be. Put yourself in the shoes of the person looking to fill a job. There is no pure science of hiring, no way of ever knowing for sure if the candidate is going to work out. Hiring somebody is a judgment call. Some executives call it a craps shoot. You hire the person you *think* is the best prospect, and you expect to be wrong some of the time. Indeed, one of the most troubling problems in industry today is the vast amounts of time and money wasted on the training and breaking in of employees who don't pan out.

So, if you are sitting on the other side of the desk doing the interviewing instead of being interviewed, you're looking mainly for assurances that the person can do the job. And what could be more reliable indication of this than the fact that the person has already done this job, or a similar job, and done it well?

Credentials, keep in mind, represent what you've *done*, not what you think you can do. Any job you've actually held is a credential, although not necessarily a credential that will mean something in a specific job situation. Advanced degrees are credentials. So are licenses. Anything concrete that in and of itself indicates you've done something can be seen as a credential.

The importance of credentials will vary enormously from job to job and from company to company. Generally speaking, the bigger and more bureaucratic a company is, the more important credentials become. Using credentials as the prevailing criteria in hiring reduces the need for people to make decisions based on intangibles. It gets people off the hook. A personnel executive who works for one of the major weekly news magazines admits that no matter how good a writer a candidate may be, he, as the personnel executive, is reluctant to set up interviews for that candidate unless the writer has already "proven himself" somewhere. "If I recommend somebody without great credentials and this person doesn't work out," he says, "I'm under the gun to justify the decision. But if the person has credentials, I can always say, 'Well, he or she looked great on paper.' "

So how do you get around credentials if you don't have them? In some cases, you don't. You accept the fact that in certain situations, if your background doesn't meet the specifications a company has set down, your chances are slim—regardless of how well you might in fact be able to do the job. You're in the same position as a highly intelligent high school student who's having trouble getting into college because of a poor performance on the SAT exams. You look elsewhere.

Often, though, you can get around the credentials bind. First of all, learn to differentiate between a hard and a flexible credentials policy. If a job ad calls for an "absolute minimum of five years experience" in a particular job, you can still get a hearing if your background is reasonably close to this. But you have more flexibility when the requirements are somewhat more vague—using terms like "strong" or "extensive" experience.

Falsifying credentials is never a good idea. Apart from the inherent immorality and illegality of it, credentials are the easiest thing to check up on. If you lack credentials but feel you have the ability to do a particular job, it is best to be scrupulously honest in your résumé, then call attention to your ability in the covering letter.

But, again, a credential has to reflect accomplishment. Let's say you're applying for a job as an advertising salesperson on a magazine. The requirement here is "at least two years experience on a magazine." You've just graduated from college so you have no experience, but you sold space for your college newspaper.

You could say, in the letter that accompanies your résumé: "I know I have the ability to sell advertising space." But this is not a credential, it's a claim. You could also say: "I sold advertising space for my college newspaper for two years." This is a credential, but not a very strong one. Or you could also say, assuming it's the truth: "In the two years that I sold advertising space for my college newspaper, ad revenues increased by nearly 100 percent." Now *that's* a credential.

The rule here is simple. When you are coming up with a

list of your own credentials, and certainly when you're presenting those credentials to a would-be employer, be as specific as possible and stress the *accomplishment* aspect of each credential.

One last point. Credentials, as I've already said, hold more sway with larger companies than with smaller companies. But if you can gain access to the ultimate hiring authority in a large company, you'll have a much stronger chance of getting some credentials waived. Sometimes it's worth a shot.

Skills: You May Have More Than You Think

"I'm really not qualified to do much of anything" is a complaint I've heard frequently from job hunters, particularly women who've been out of the job market raising a family. Yet I've never met anybody who didn't have at least *one* marketable skill. There are, of course, different types of skills, ranging from the highly technical to the general. The ability to operate a complicated piece of technical equipment is a skill, but so is the ability to organize a successful fundraiser for a charity or social group. Typing, taking shorthand, playing a musical instrument, knowing a foreign language—these are all marketable skills. But so is the ability to tell stories to young children in a captivating way.

Much of what I said earlier about credentials applies as well to skills. The importance of skills will vary from job to job and from company to company. Some companies are so adamant about skill requirements they'll insist that you take some sort of test. Other companies, if they are impressed with you, may waive a skill requirement, on the understanding that you'll undergo special training. Here again, the smaller and more loosely structured the company, the more flexible the policy.

It makes no sense to misrepresent the level of your skills: you'll be found out soon enough. But if you think you're reasonably close to the skill requirements set down in a particular job situation, follow the same advice I gave earlier on for credentials. Be honest in your résumé, but draw attention to what you think makes your situation unique. "It's true," you might say, "that I've never designed book jackets. But I've designed record album covers and the same basic principles apply."

Your Personal Assets: Don't Underestimate Them

"Qualifications are important," said one of the respondents in our Burke survey, "but it's the *whole* person I'm interested in. How does that person come across? How enthusiastic is this person. How *positive* is this person—that's so important."

The comment typifies those we received in our survey, and it helps explain one of the more interesting findings in the survey—one that suggests that most personnel executives and most top management executives will overlook job experience (within reason, of course) if you impress them enough with your personal assets, your potential.

Again, your personal assets may not be enough in many situations to overcome your shortcomings in job experience and skills. But, at the same time, personal qualities can keep you in the running. They can give you the edge over candidates who may outdistance you in qualifications but not in personal assets.

Consider the case of a statistician I once knew whom we'll call Jane. Well, she used to be a statistician. Jane was one of twelve statisticians working for a Wall Street brokerage firm, but she was not a very good statistician and the company decided she had to go.

There was only one problem. Jane was one heck of an employee—dependable, prompt, pleasant to be around, a very hard worker. So what did the company do? At the meeting when the officers were making up their mind to fire Jane, they decided instead to train her to become a registered "rep"—a job that paid more money and had a better future. As one of the officers explained to me: "You get an employee like her once in a blue moon. We *had* to find a place for her."

Jane is only one of many examples I could cite to show

how important personality factors can be when you're looking for a job. Years ago our company was asked by a large advertising agency to find an executive to head their financial division. They insisted they wanted somebody with an extensive background in advertising. But one day a man whose last job had been with the U.S. government came into our office. He impressed me so much with his intelligence, his confidence, and his worldliness that I called the agency president and told him I had a person I thought he should see, never mind the fact that he'd never worked in advertising. The man got the job.

So, if you haven't already done so, take an inventory of your personal assets with a special eye toward what employers are looking for. Be alert to your strengths, but don't overlook your weaknesses—the things about you that might discourage a potential employer from hiring you.

To help you take this inventory, I've drawn up a list of the characteristics and traits that our surveys have found count the most in most job situations. In each case, my chief concern is how these traits affect the hiring decision. It's up to you to evaluate yourself in every area and, on the basis of this evaluation, to take the steps suggested.

Your Appearance

It is a reasonable assumption, based on the findings of our surveys, that within the first two minutes of any personal meeting with somebody who has the power to hire you or screen you out, the decision has pretty much been made. That's how strongly first impressions affect the hiring decision, and this is why the way you look is so important to your job search strategy.

Let me point out quickly here, before you get the wrong idea, that you don't have to look like a movie star in order to make a "favorable" first impression. Our surveys show that less than 5 percent of personnel directors consider physical attractiveness "very important" in a hiring decision. Some studies show, in fact, that exceptionally attractive people, particularly attractive women, may be at something of a disadvantage in certain job situations. "It's a prejudice, I admit," is how one personnel director puts it. "But I'm hesitant to hire a woman who is *too* pretty because I figure somebody is going to come along and marry her very quickly. Besides, if a woman is really good-looking, she's going to disrupt the office environment. The men in the office won't pay enough attention to their work."

But let's not overstate the case. All things considered, it's better to be exceptionally attractive than exceptionally unattractive. Why should it matter in most job situations? Well, it shouldn't, but we're all guilty of making judgments and drawing conclusions about a person simply on the basis of the way he or she looks or is dressed. I know of situations in which a candidate has been turned down because the interviewer took exception to his beard. I know of personnel executives who won't hire redheads. And our survey indicates that as many as 75 percent of personnel executives will bypass a substantially overweight candidate in favor of a thinner, similarly qualified candidate.

It gives me no pleasure to make this point. Prejudice is prejudice whether it is based on race or religion or weight or height or anything that has no true bearing on a person's ability to do a particular job. Worse, while there are legal sanctions designed to control job discrimination on the basis of religion, age, sex, and race, there isn't much legal protection for somebody who is losing out because he or she is too homely, or doesn't dress in a manner that impresses the interviewer.

The problem here, of course, isn't so much that you *are* a certain way, but that certain aspects of your appearance will lead people to make conclusions about you, whether these conclusions are justified or not (and they're usually not). I once went on the *To Tell the Truth* television show as the *real* Robert Half. I was defending the rights of fat people, who are often unjustly discriminated against. Talking to the producers ahead of time, I was surprised to learn that in the sixteen years the show had been on the air, panel members had failed to choose the person who was telling the truth nearly two thirds of the time. Think of it: there are only three people to choose from, and most of the people on the panel are "experts," who've been making choices for years. This shows you how much people can be influenced by personality and appearance. To be fat, in the eyes of many people, is to be lazy and unhealthy; to be short, in the eyes of others, is to be hostile and pushy. Simply being a woman, to the typical male chauvinist, means to be "fragile" and "emotional."

These stereotypes are maddening, but you can deal with them only up to a point. A heavy-set accountant I once placed in a good job knew that some interviewers were going to judge him as being lethargic and unhealthy, so he went out of his way in the interview to emphasize what a hard worker he was and how good an attendance record he'd had at his last job. He also wore a pinstripe suit to give him a more streamlined look.

Now there is a slight danger here that in being overly sensitive to what your interviewer's reaction might be, you overdo your counterattacking strategy. In other words, if you try to convince an interviewer how healthy you are, you can end up making the interviewer suspect there must be something wrong with you. Otherwise, why would you appear so defensive?

All of which brings up a basic dilemma when it comes to appearance. On the one hand, you want your appearance to be your attempt to look a certain way that you end up beating yourself at your own game.

There are two general approaches to the problem. One is simply not to worry about your appearance, other than to meet basic, generally accepted standards for cleanliness, neatness, and good grooming. In other words, you don't change your normal appearance—the way you dress, comb your hair, etc.—just because you're applying for a job.

The advantage of this strategy is that it's easy to carry out: you don't have to work at it. The disadvantage, though, is that what is "normal" for you may trigger, for no logical reason, a negative response from the interviewer. Let's take an extreme. Let's say you're a man who likes to dress Western style, in jeans and boots. Maybe in some companies, nobody cares how you dress; the person who interviews you might even be wearing jeans and boots. But one survey I know of shows that executives would have a negative response if either a man or a woman walked into an interview wearing jeans, even in this day of high-priced designer jeans.

You can't control the quirks of the people who have to pass judgment on you. What's normal and comfortable for you may not be normal and comfortable for them. You see nothing wrong with wearing jeans and boots, but they see you as an oddball, somebody who might not fit in. You win the battle of self-determination: you do your own thing. Somebody else gets the job.

The second strategy—and the one I recommend—is to follow the old adage: When in Rome, do as the Romans do. Play it safe. Avoid extremes. In every facet of appearance, there are certain norms, and you're always better off staying within these norms—at least until you're hired. It may have been okay in your last job to wear your hair (if you're a man) at almost shoulder length, but now that you're in the job market, bite the bullet and get it cut shorter. By the same token (and again if you're a man) if you've always favored a fifties-style crew cut and you're in the job market now, let your hair grow. The same rule applies to women: stick to what is unlikely to draw attention.

Follow the same guidelines in every facet of your appearance, especially when it comes to your clothes. I'll go into clothing a little later on in this chapter, but for now it's enough to say that what is trendy and stylish according to *Vogue* or *Gentlemen's Quarterly* isn't necessarily appropriate for a job interview. If you're going to err, do so on the side of conservatism. Dress for a job interview as if you were going to a bank to ask for a loan.

Be Comfortable with How You Look

Few of us always look as good as we would like to look, but most of us don't do enough with those aspects of our appearance over which we have a good deal of control. And *these* features—your basic grooming, your posture, your clothing, your weight, and the general image you project—are the things that will count most in shaping the attitudes of your interviewers one way or another. If there is a general guideline here, it is this: *Don't force it.* Avoid extremes (too much makeup, a bizarre hairstyle, way-out clothing, etc.). Avoid the common trap of working so hard to conceal some feature of your appearance that you succeed only in drawing more attention to it.

Some specifics:

Your hair. It's the first thing most people notice about you, so keep it clean and have it cut or styled regularly during your job search. Never put anything on your hair that makes it look very shiny or greasy. If you have a dandruff problem, get it under control, and in the meanwhile, don't wear dark clothing.

Are you dyeing it? Covering up or downplaying the gray in your hair will obviously make you look younger, which could help you in some situations. But if you're going to do it—and I, for one, would never advise strongly that you do it—have it done professionally and use restraint. If the wrinkles on your face say you're fifty and the color of your hair says twenty-five, you'll look artificial.

I feel the same way about men wearing hairpieces. Unless you're willing to invest enough money to get a hairpiece that doesn't *look* like a hairpiece, don't waste your money. If an interviewer suspects you're wearing one, it could hurt your chances. You also run the risk that an interviewer will be so distracted by his or her curiosity (they're wondering whether or not the hair is yours) that it interferes with your presentation. For what it's worth, I spend a good deal of time with the top executives of many of the country's largest corporations, and in no case could having gray or white hair, or being bald or nearly bald, be called an obstacle to success.

Your skin. Your complexion is important, but mainly in terms of what it says about the general state of your health.

Regardless of the color of your skin, if you spend a reasonable amount of time outdoors every day, it will have a fairly healthy glow. I know of a few male executives who wear a touch of makeup, but it's a risky business unless you know how to use it and are absolutely certain that no one can detect it.

Cosmetic Surgery. A woman bank executive I heard of recently swears that the best thing she ever did for her career was to have her nose made smaller two years ago. A New York advertising executive insists that he owes his present job to the plastic surgeon who took care of the heavy bags under his eyes. Am I advocating plastic surgery as a strategy for getting hired? Hardly, but I'm not ruling it out, either. The benefits most people get from plastic surgery are more indirect than direct. People who ''correct'' what they have long considered a defect feel better about themselves and, as a consequence, handle themselves with more assurance in interviews and similar situations.

View plastic surgery as an option but not a priority. Within reason, most of the facial features that people feel self-conscious about are more worrisome to them than to those they come into contact with. I myself take notice of little things like skin blotches or warts or unusually heavy bags only if the person I'm talking to gives me the feeling that he or she is self-conscious about it; and, even then, it doesn't sway my opinion one way or the other. But if something about your appearance bothers you so much that it diverts your attention away from what you should be concentrating on when you're dealing with people, and if that problem can be corrected without too much expense or risk to your health, then by all means explore the possibility. The more comfortable about your appearance you are, the more overall confidence you will generate. And confidence, in the end, is more important than appearance.

Your height and weight. First, the bad news. Everything else being equal, your chances of getting hired for most good jobs are better if you are tall and slim than if you are short and fat. Any number of studies bear this out, including our own. One study, conducted at the University of Pittsburgh, indicates that the taller you are, the higher the starting salary you're likely to get.

Let's not get overly paranoid about these studies. First of all height is generally not a problem area for women. And men have to be noticeably shorter than average before height becomes a major handicap. Even then, if you have enough going for you, you can overcome it. Secondly, your height isn't nearly as important as the *presence* you are able to generate when you meet people. Even if you are a good deal shorter than average, you can look authoritative. Spend a little more money on your clothes. If necessary, get them custom tailored. Wear expensive-looking white shirts (the contrast between the white shirt and dark suit is important). Look people in the eye when you talk to them. Exude energy and confidence, and your height becomes secondary.

Weight, however, is a different story. Our company conducted a study in 1974 that showed there were more than four times as many fat executives in the $10,000 to $20,000 range than in the $25,000 to $45,000 range. Other studies show that a noticeably fat man or woman may have only half the chance of getting even a job interview that a normal-weight person would have.

This bias can be explained, if not defended. Forgetting the pure appearance aspect, a lot of employers equate being fat with being lazy or unhealthy. Obesity is also seen, by many people, as a sign that the person lacks self-discipline or has some psychological problem that could interfere with his or her ability to do the job.

If you yourself are *noticeably* overweight (and being 5 to 10 pounds too heavy is *not*, in my judgment, being noticeably overweight), you have one of two options. The first and most obvious is to go on a diet, which is healthy advice regardless of your job status. Secondly, recognize the fact that your obesity may be working against you. Don't mention your weight problem: you may create the impression that you're obsessed by it. Work to counteract the prejudicial notion that because you are overweight, you are a lazy, undisciplined, or unhealthy person. Stress your attendance record at your last job (assuming it's worth stressing). Guard against appearing too lethargic.

What You Wear

I've already touched briefly on how important the clothes you wear when you meet prospective employers can be in the impression you create; but the subject is important enough to warrant more elaboration. Few of us like to admit it, but we *are* influenced by the way people are dressed, even though it's a superficial method by which to judge a person. Ultimately, of course, you have to dress in a way that complements your build, your coloring and, in some respects, your personality. But here are some general tips to keep in mind as you're aiming toward this objective:

1. *Spend as much as you can afford on quality clothing.* You are better off with two or three expensive-looking outfits than with five or six cheap-looking outfits. There are enough outlet-type clothing stores around today that offer solid, up-to-date name-brand clothing, but you have to know your way around them. If you don't know much about clothing, ask a friend who is a clotheshorse to help you get what you need.

2. *Be careful of any clothing item that "types" you.* An example for men would be a blazer with a school emblem. Another would be a Western-style outfit.

3. *When in doubt, be conservative.* Avoid severely tailored styles, overly bold colors, overly busy patterns. No ascots, please.

4. *Go easy on the jewelry.* Women should keep it simple. Men: avoid any jewelry that is not functional, and don't wear any item that might be considered feminine.

5. *Don't stint on your shoes.* To spend big dollars on a suit and buy the least expensive shoes you can find is like ordering a Rolls Royce with vinyl upholstery. I've heard of doormen in exclusive New York City restaurants who insist they can gauge the size of the tips they're going to get by the shoes a person is wearing.

6. *Be extra careful of the tailoring.* No clothes will look really good on you, regardless of how expensive they are, if they don't fit you perfectly.

How Healthy You Are

Being in good health will not, in and of itself, get you hired. But any impression you give that you're *not* in the best of health is a red flag that signals heavily against you. I feel so strongly about this point, I have counseled many candidates to postpone interviews when they felt the slightest bit under the weather. Apart from not looking your best when not feeing well, it's difficult to give a job interview performance under these conditions.

Your Personality Traits

Take a look at the form on page 214. It's a variation of a standard form used by many companies today to evaluate the character traits of potential employees. Depending on the job, of course, certain character traits take on more importance than others. But most of the traits listed on this form are going to figure, one way or another, in the hiring decision. Let's look at these traits in order to see why employers consider them important and the basis on which you're being judged in each instance.

Dependability. "I want somebody I can count on" is a refrain I have heard thousands of times throughout my career. It seems a simple enough requirement, and yet the fear that you might *not* be dependable could easily get you eliminated from consideration. Dependability, of course, means your ability to show up for work every day on time, to do the job you're supposed to do with a minimum of supervision, to allow your supervisor or boss the luxury of knowing that when you say you're going to do something, you'll get it done.

The importance that employers attach to dependability explains why it is so essential for you to be punctual for appointments. You don't have all that many ways before you start work to demonstrate dependability, so anything you do that suggests otherwise can do nothing but hurt your chances. Try to make sure your references mention how dependable you are. And it doesn't hurt at all, in interviews, to call attention to your dependability as one of your major assets. Frequently in a job interview someone is going to ask you to talk briefly about your assets. I was always impressed by people who came right out and said: "Well, one thing I'd have to say is that if you give me a job to do, you can be sure it's going to get done."

And if you're still not convinced that dependability is an important asset, listen to a story the vice president of public relations for a soft drink company likes to tell. It seems that earlier in his career, he was up for a job he wanted badly and had an interview set for a Saturday morning in the hotel suite of the executives who were evaluating candidates. As luck would have it, that Saturday morning produced one of the worst rain storms in memory—a near hurricane. Even so, the man showed up for the interview and even apologized for being ten minutes late.

"Why would you try to come up here in this terrible weather?" one of the interviewers asked him.

"Because," the man replied, "I said I would *be* here."

He got the job.

Stability. How well do you deal with pressure? Does it bring out the best in you or do you get jumpy and nervous? Certain jobs have more built-in pressure than others, but your general stability is on the mind of everyone who has to pass judgment on you. It's possible, in fact, that at some time during the interview process, an interviewer will do things or say things deliberately designed to test your emotional stability.

One barometer of stability is your employment record to date. If you haven't stayed at any one job for any substantial length of time, your stability will become suspect and you'll have to address yourself to this suspicion during an interview. Otherwise, it's your basic manner and the way you respond in an interview that's going to indicate your degree of innate stability to the interviewer. Allowances will be made for the fact that you're a little nervous or anxious in the interview, but signs of nervousness or tension that go beyond the norm will raise troublesome questions. "I'm afraid to take a chance with that man (woman) you sent me yesterday," I've heard a client say too many times. "There's something about that person that worries me."

Who's to say what that "something" could be? Maybe it was some nervous habit the candidate had? Maybe it was a way of laughing? Maybe the person talked too loudly, or too softly? I've had clients complain that a candidate appeared *too* calm in an interview.

Another way you reflect your emotional stability—or lack thereof—is in your dealings with receptionists and secretaries. Justified as you might be, never bully or lose your temper with anybody you deal with when you're job searching. More executives than you might imagine will ask their secretaries to give a general impression of you once you've been through the interview. The secretary doesn't have the power to get you hired, but your chances for getting the job aren't going to be helped if you're described as being "difficult" or "abusive."

The likelihood is that stability won't be a problem in your particular case. All the same, here are some of the factors that interviewers tend to equate with a candidate who may have a stability problem:

1. *Any behavior in the extreme.* Being either unusually animated or unusually stiff. Talking much too much or not talking at all. Smiling too much or not smiling at all.

2. *The inability to stay focused on one point or one question.* You hop around from point to point without clearly expressing yourself, without making any sense.

3. *Disorganization that goes well beyond the norm.* General scatterbrainedness—not being able to locate papers in your briefcase or to find a pen in your purse. (I heard of an instance in which a woman dumped the entire contents of her purse on the desk of the man interviewing her in order to find a card she was looking for.)

4. *Unresponsiveness.* You've heard the phrase "like talking to a stone wall." Don't be one.

Honesty. I mention honesty here because there's a temptation when you're looking for work either to lie outright or to misrepresent your accomplishments. Candidates rationalize that since they are lying only to get the job, the lie can be justified.

There are problems with this reasoning. First, the lies you tell, even if believed, may not get you the job. Secondly, if it becomes apparent—and it often does when you misrepresent yourself—that you can't perform in the job in the way you led your employer to believe, you'll most likely be fired on the spot.

Incidentally, you never mention the fact that you're honest. It's *assumed.* Mention your honesty, and you create the suspicion that you might not be. (Will Richard Nixon ever live down the fact that he once said, "I am not a crook"?)

Drive. As long as you don't give off the impression that you'd shoot your grandmother to further your career, you can't go wrong in most job interview situations by showing drive and ambition. And it's easier than you might think to give the impression that you *lack* these characteristics. Our survey shows clearly that interviewers like to see assertiveness and aggressiveness in job candidates.

But you have to do more than simply verbalize your desire

to achieve. For one thing, your résumé is going to make clear just how much of a go-getter you really are. If your work experience to date shows no unusually rapid advancement, don't expect any pronouncements you make on the subject to have much impact.

You demonstrate determination and drive by *action:* by going into a job interview, for instance, armed with facts and figures about the company considering you, filled with ideas on how you might be able to help that company. The fact that you've gone to the trouble of assembling this information says something about you: you are more ambitious than the average person, with more drive to succeed. You won't have to verbalize it.

Another way you indicate drive is by asking questions during an interview that relate indirectly to the company's promotion policies. You ask, in passing, how old the executive vice president is, which gives the impression that you're thinking ahead but doesn't suggest that you're not interested in the job at hand. You mention, when the subject comes up, not how ambitious you are, but how seriously you take your career and your job. If you're asked to describe a weakness, you might "confess" that sometimes you set goals for yourself that are too high.

We'll get into more of interview strategy in Chapter V, but keep in mind for now that your desire to "get ahead" is an asset to you as a job candidate. Don't underplay it.

Personability. If your track record is strong enough, and if what you have to offer is something a company needs badly enough, your ability to get along with people may have little if any bearing at all on the hiring decision. But don't push your luck! Nobody is going to hire you because you *can't* get along with people, and most companies will pass you over if your personality seems objectionable. I've yet to see a personnel evaluation form that didn't have a section devoted to personability.

There is no great art in being personable. Even if you're shy—and most people are—it's easy. It's a matter of simple courtesy and tact. It's being responsive when people approach you. It's being helpful when the need arises. It's showing basic consideration. It's having—and not being afraid to use—something we all have: a smile. And don't think that because your particular job specialty doesn't involve much interaction with people, your personality doesn't matter. It does. As objective as the person responsible for hiring you is, he or she is still going to rely, in part, on his or her personal reaction to you. It is no coincidence that most of the truly successful people I know are not only good at what they do but very decent, pleasant people as well.

Loyalty. Nobody in a hiring position will condemn you for wanting to get ahead, but give someone the slightest hint that you don't put much value on loyalty, and your chances of getting hired become slim indeed. Forget the double standard here which says that it's "healthy ambition" when your boss goes with another company but "disloyalty" when you do the same thing. Resign yourself to the rules of the game. The rules state simply that thou shalt praise the virtues of loyalty.

Your record, of course, will give some indication of how loyal you actually are. It's tough to preach loyalty in the face of a record that shows you've worked for six different companies over the past five years. But even if your résumé paints you as in no way disloyal, there are ways in which you might inadvertently arouse suspicion. The easiest is to say unflattering things about a former employer or former boss (no matter how justified you may be in your comments). I heard recently of an executive who based his pitch to a company on the fact that he'd worked for the company's chief competitor and knew their "weaknesses." He didn't get the job. Why? Because, as the executive who turned him down explained to me, "Who's to say this guy won't leave us in a year or two and make the same offer to one of *our* competitors?"

Responsibility. Can you assume responsibility? Don't be in too much of a hurry to answer this because the ability to take on responsibility is rare. There are plenty of competent and dependable people around, but not too many people who take a *personal* responsibility for the job they do. Get this quality across to the people who interview you and you'll have a leg up on most of your competitors.

One of the ways you show this sense of responsibility is by being willing to accept blame. I remember in the late 1960s interviewing a man who'd been fired from a company that had a widespread reputation for being difficult to work for. What impressed me was that this man made no excuses, even though he had plenty of justification for blaming the company. "I blew it," he said flatly. "There were some things I could have done that I didn't think to do. I can't blame them."

By the same token, you indicate a lack of responsibility by offering excuses for whatever aspects of your work background might need defending. You tell an interviewer that your last company was "very disorganized," or "never really utilized me to best advantage." You criticize a former employer of yours for showing "favoritism." You suggest that had the company given *you* more responsibility, it wouldn't have gotten itself into financial trouble.

I'm not suggesting here that you deliberately call attention to your failures and weaknesses. But the way you respond when asked to explain some feature of your work experience that doesn't show you off in the best of lights says more about you than you may think. The more you can show that you bring to your job a true sense of personal responsibility, that you see the success of the company you work for as part of your responsibility, that you're willing to accept the mistakes of your subordinates as your responsibility, the more attractive a candidate you will appear to the people who must evaluate you.

Determining Your Asking Price

The subject of money is going to turn up in nearly every job situation you face, so you might as well make up your mind not to be embarrassed or self-conscious when you talk about it. Give any indication to an interviewer that you're embarrassed about your salary request and you can almost bank on a *lower* offer. Your interviewers aren't going to take the subject of money personally, and neither should you.

We'll talk about actual salary negotiations in a later chapter. For now, you need some guidelines on the money you're looking for. Conventional wisdom says to find out, if possible, the maximum a company is willing to pay and then set your asking price a little bit higher. It's basic horse-trading gospel. The more you ask for, the less you have to settle for.

This advice isn't bad insofar as it goes, but it doesn't help you much in this preliminary, job-targeting phase of your search. Remember, too, that if you turn down a job offer because you're not happy with the money, you're pretty much closed to the case on that particular job. In any case, you need some salary guidelines independent of any specific situation: a ballpark figure to serve as a basis of negotiation.

The first thing you need to know is what the "going rate" is in the general target area you've set up. What are middle management financial executives making these days? How much are magazine editors making? Do some research in the library (there are books out that offer this kind of information). Read ads in the newspaper or trade magazines for additional data. You'll probably come up with a fairly broad range, and this is good because it gives you a chance to adjust your figure according to your situation. I'm going to assume that this range meets your basic living expenses. If it doesn't, you're looking in the wrong area. Get some new targets. But, assuming the salary range is something you can live with, figure in two things: one, what you were earning in your last job; and, two, the qualifications you bring to the new job situation.

In most situations, the hiring authority will base the offer you ultimately get on both the company's salary range and your previous earnings, your qualifications and, if they want you badly enough, what they think it might take to hire you. Remember, though, that no matter how badly a company wants you, you're unlikely to be offered any *more* than your counterparts at the firm.

Let's figure that the company's range for a particular job is between $25,000 and $30,000. They'd like to pay $25,000. They'll go as high as $30,000 for a blue chipper. Now, assuming your qualifications are strong and you were making, say, $27,000 a year on your last job, you can expect an offer close to $30,000. If, on the other hand, you were only earning $20,000 a year in your last job, you'll probably have a tough time getting more than $25,000—regardless of your qualifications.

If you think it's unfair that your salary demands have to be predicated, not so much on how good you are, but on what you were earning in your last job, you're right. But that's how most people in the corporate world think. Like it or not, people will equate your contribution to a company by how much they paid you. You may have been the best office supervisor in the industry, but the fact that you were earning a good $5,000 a year less than other office supervisors in the same industry will worry a would-be employer. The suspicion will be that you're not worth more. You may get a chance, but you'll have to start at the lower figure and work your way up. My advice is not to fight the system but to join it.

Some job hunters tend to *increase* their salary demands in proportion to the length of time they're out of work. The logic is that now they have more economic ground to make up. I call this Half's Inverse Law of Successful Job Changing, and I urge you not to get caught up in it. Your attractiveness as a job candidate is not proportionate to the amount of time you've been out of work. If anything, it may diminish. If you were trying to sell a house and it had been on the market for six months without a bid, you wouldn't *raise* the price. So, if anything, you should be prepared, as time goes on, to reduce your salary demands somewhat.

Which brings up a crucial point: the role your financial situation plays in your job decisions. If you have enough money in reserve to wait out the offer you're looking for, fine. Be as independent as you like; but be aware, too, that your reserve can thin out quickly. The higher your salary requirements, the more you limit your chances. It would be nice to get more money in your next job, but if you have no job, smart money says to look for a lateral change.

The reason for this is pure arithmetic. Let's say you were earning $25,000 a year in your last job—about $481 a week. You get fired, and you figure that now is the time to up your salary demands, to $30,000—a 20 percent increase, or about $93 a week. It's a basic axiom in our business that job hunters looking to make a lateral move (that is, to a job that carries no major increase in salary) can generally expect to get a new job within a month or two of intelligent job hunting. Job hunters looking for a 20 percent increase, on the other hand, often take up to six months to find a position with this kind of an increase, and, at that, many of them have to settle for a lower salary. Remember, a company can often fill from within for a lower salary, even if they give their employee an increase.

Let's assume your six-month search is successful. You get a job that pays you $30,000 and you feel like drinking a toast to victory. Count me out. Based on the scenario I've just described, you've lost 22 weeks of salary at $481, which amounts to more than $10,500, less unemployment insurance. Forgetting, even, about income tax, it's going to take you nearly two years to make up the difference with your new salary. With those kind of victories, you can't afford too many defeats.

Avoiding the "Faceless Candidate" Trap

Probably the toughest hiring situation of all comes about when you've been fired with hundreds and maybe more from your firm. Suddenly the local job race is crowded and, worse, crowded with people who, from the employer's point of view, all fit pretty much the same mold. So, rather than try to hire the best person from a company that has just laid off a great many people, some interviewers won't hire anybody from that company.

Here's what to do:

1. *Consider out of town.* The idea may not appeal to you. Your family might not be happy. But it's an option that deserves serious consideration. In a mass layoff situation, your chances of getting hired out of town are always greater than they are if you stay put.

2. *Write a functional résumé.* Instead of listing the company first, stress your responsibilities and accomplishments. And when you write your covering letter, don't give the name of the company you've just been asked to leave. Don't even mention the industry. Simply put "large manufacturing firm," or some such description.

3. *Don't think small.* You think "small" when you say to yourself you can only do one or two things well. Suppose you were in the technical department of your firm. Do you have a nice personality? Do you get along well with people? Are you a hard worker? Maybe you could *sell* technical products.

4. *Ask for a chance.* I see nothing wrong, as I mention several times in this book, with asking for a job on a trial basis—to prove to the employer that you can handle it. It won't always work, but your chances of getting a job are better when you show a willingness to prove yourself than when you sit back and wait for guarantees.

If You've Been a Job-Jumper . . .

I once interviewed a candidate who had had nearly fifty jobs in twenty years. "I'm actually very stable," he said. "I've never quit a job."

He had a point. Not a great point from the aspect of most interviewers, but a point, anyway. Having a résumé that's filled with job after job could be a hindrance to you, especially if you're looking into a company that prides itself on its stable atmosphere. On the other hand, if you've had a lot of jobs, you probably have a lot of experience at *getting* jobs, in which case you probably don't need this book.

The main thing to keep in mind if you have a background that is filled with a lot of jobs is to concentrate on "fast-track" companies—the companies that are known for hiring people with diversified experience, companies accustomed to taking people from outside the industry. Fortunately, these are the companies that usually get written about the most in the major business publications. Spend a couple of hours in the library with back issues of magazines like *Fortune*, *Business Week*, *Barrons*, and *Financial World*, and you'll come up with a list of a dozen or so of these companies. Then take it from there.

IV

Putting "Sell" into Your Résumé

*Interviewers want to know about your past so
they can project your future.*

If you think *preparing* a résumé is a chore, consider the poor person who has to read it. Remember, you have only one résumé to worry about, but a typical job opening advertised in the Sunday paper might draw as many as five hundred applications. And the typical personnel executive for a large firm has to screen for dozens of jobs at any given time, not to mention all the other headaches related to his or her job. I once asked the director of personnel of a major cosmetics firm how much time in an average day he spent reading over résumés. "As little time as possible," he said.

You can't blame him. I sat down with a calculator and estimated that if one thousand personnel executives did nothing else but read and evaluate all the résumés currently in circulation, it would take each of them an average of seventy-one years, and that's figuring on no more than four minutes per résumé. I also figured out, based on my estimates, that if you took all the résumés in circulation at the present time and laid them end to end, they would circle the circumference of the earth nearly fifteen times.

Now we come to *your* résumé.

It's out there (presumably) with hundreds of other résumés, maybe on a desk somewhere in the middle of a pile of three hundred. You may have spent the better part of a week sweating over it, asking advice, getting people to read it, changing the format, shifting around words—*and it may not even get read*. Somebody might just give it a brief once-over and toss it into the pile marked "Reject." That quick.

So now you know the enemy: numbers. Your résumé against all those other résumés out there. How do you make sure it gets a reading? How do you keep it from being tossed into the reject pile?

We're going to look into all of these questions in this chapter, but first I want to emphasize that for all the résumés out there and for all the displeasure personnel people and other executives in hiring positions have in reading them, you *need* a solid résumé. It's your admission ticket into the job race. True, you may not need it *all* the time. In some situations, you may even try to get along without it. But most of the time, you're going to have to produce one. And while a résumé may not necessarily *get* you the job—indeed, it usually won't, on its *own*—a poorly prepared résumé can knock you out of the running. And the worst part of losing a job because of a weak résumé is that the résumé is the one aspect of your job search over which you are in complete control. If your résumé doesn't show you off in the best light, it's nobody's fault but your own.

Resumania

A résumé is more than a list of particulars relating to your job experience. It is an advertisement for yourself—a selling piece that has to shout out to whoever reads it: "I am somebody who warrants your serious consideration. You'll be making a big mistake if you don't give me an interview."

Sounds simple enough, doesn't it? Yet most of the résumés that have come across my desk throughout my career—and I couldn't begin to estimate how many—haven't done this. Indeed, more than a few of the résumés that have crossed my desk have had the opposite effect. They have warned me *against* moving the candidate along to the next step. Here are some choice examples from my private file of what I call Resumania:

Besides keeping my wife and five kids happy, I enjoy a good game of chess, a good symphony and a good dry martini . . .

I am impatient with quibbling over minor details. I am stubborn on matters of principle and major objectives. I dislike routine, ultra-conservative or defensive thinking, unnecessary jobs, inefficient systems and Republicans.

My hobbies are solitaire, chess, music, golf, golf, and more golf.

My objective is to find a position with an organization beset with a variety of problems while simultaneously beginning to stir with the fever of acquisitions and diversification. As the nature of the job declines in the hierarchy of preference, so obviously would come into play the decisiveness of compensating subordinate factors.

The company I am looking to work for must be willing to put a new man into its organization who will step on toes and make many management people mad. However, they must be looking for a man who makes friends easily.

My diploma register number is 9579; my employee number was 16982 at Denver. My employee number in Des Moines is 882431. I was staff sergeant E-6. I instructed course 70c20.

Each of the examples above came from actual résumés. They gave me something to chuckle over, something to add to my Resumania file. They didn't help the cause of the job candidate responsible for them.

I have scores of other résumés on file from candidates who probably had no idea their résumés were knocking them out of the running. Résumés that run for five pages. Résumés that consist of one short paragraph. Résumés that are filled with misspellings. Résumés that are sloppily typed and filled with little chicken scratches impossible to read. Résumés that are simply incomprehensible.

Your résumé should never end up in this file—not if you follow some of the simple suggestions I'm going to offer you in this chapter.

How Good Is Your Current Résumé?

If you already have a résumé, get it out. Read it through. Then answer the following questions:

1. Is it letter-perfect?

2. Is it photo offset on a substantial-looking 8½″ × 11″ bond paper?

3. Does it look good (not too much material jammed together)?

4. Is it easy to read and follow?

5. Is it easy to understand? (That is, does it make its points clearly and concisely?)

6. Do you get a feeling, when reading it, of *accomplishment*?

7. Does it reflect the tone and the feel you want it to reflect?

8. Is it the best possible résumé you could prepare?

If you answered no to any of the above questions, you need a new résumé.

What Your Résumé Must Do

First, the basics:

A résumé has to be letter-perfect, neat, easy to read. It should generally be no more than two pages long. It should be well organized.

So much for the easy part.

The hard part is *putting that résumé to work,* making it do as much as a résumé can do. Making it a successful sales device. I don't care how well organized, how neat, how smoothly written your résumé is, if it doesn't have any "sell" in it, it's not doing its job.

And what is a "selling" résumé? It's a résumé that *gives the person who reads it a reason to call you in for an interview.* It's a résumé that showcases everything you have to offer in the most positive light, yet without strain. This is a tricky balance to achieve, but you can do it.

Professional Help: Is It Worth It?

If you want, you can find people who specialize in helping job seekers to prepare résumés—who, in fact, *do* the actual preparation. Some of them charge several hundred to several thousand dollars for the service.

The temptation to call up on such a service (particularly if you can afford it) is obvious. After all, why risk things? Why not turn the whole burdensome matter over to a "professional"?

Resist the temptation. Forgetting the money (which, by the way, might be better spent on a new suit or dress), there isn't too much a résumé "specialist" can do that you can't do for yourself—with a little thought and effort. If you can think logically and if you are of average intelligence, you can prepare your own résumé, and do it probably as well, even better, than a professional.

I have other reasons, apart from the money, for steering you away from the professional résumé writing services. For one thing, professionally written résumés often have an assembly-line look. I can usually spot them at a glance, and so can any experienced hiring executive. Some personnel directors as a matter of policy automatically eliminate from consideration résumés that look to have been professionally done.

But there's an even more important reason for working on your résumé yourself. Doing so forces you to examine yourself, helps to give you a sense of just what you have to offer a prospective employer. It prepares you, in other words, for many of the situations you're going to run into when you go to interviews. Putting together your own résumé helps you to appreciate aspects about yourself, or your job background, that you may not have been aware of before. You get to know the product better. You become a better salesperson.

If you want to consult with an employment adviser or a counselor who's been recommended to you, fine. If you want the résumé professionally edited, that's okay, too. And, by all means, have your résumé professionally typed and run off—offset, if possible. But do the actual preparation and the writing of the résumé yourself.

The Basics

We'll get to the writing in a moment, but first let's look at some of the general principles of résumé preparation:

1. *Be brief and to the point*. A résumé is not an autobiography, nor a forum for your personal philosophies. Stick to the facts. Never express in four or five words what can be said in two or three.

2. *Avoid the pronoun "I."* The résumé is obviously about you, so you don't ever have to mention yourself in the first person, except perhaps in an objective statement at the end, or where it becomes awkward to leave it out.

3. *Include only relevant information*. Your spouse's name, the names of your children (and your dog), the name of the grammar school you went to—none of these things has anything to do with your ability to work for the company you're applying to. Omit them, and anything else that isn't directly connected to your employment experience, your education beyond high school, and personal information that would be of interest to an employer.

4. *Stress what you've accomplished*. It isn't enough to mention the position you held in previous jobs, or even your responsibilities and duties. Give the person who reads your résumé a sense of what you accomplished and what you

contributed to the success of every company or organization you've worked for.

5. *Don't be cute or chatty.* A résumé is not the place to get folksy or cute. Keep the tone on an even, straightforward, businesslike level.

6. *Keep your sentences short.* Express yourself in short, concise sentences. A good rule is to start as many sentences as possible with an active word.

7. *Toot your own horn—but softly.* Maybe you did "save the company from going under." Say it more diplomatically. Example: "Created financial plan that helped increase productivity."

8. *Don't list salary or references, and don't include a photograph.* You can talk salary in your covering letter. You can give references on request. You can show the company what you look like when you get interviewed.

9. *Don't mention anything blatantly negative.* Candor is an admirable quality, but don't go overboard on your résumé. Don't lie, but don't get bogged down for example in the reasons you had to leave a particular job.

10. *Don't mention race or religion.* Or membership in organizations that might indicate race or religion. It's not that you're hiding anything, but why take a chance that the person who first gets your résumé is a bigot?

One final basic: Don't expect one résumé to do the job that three or four different résumés might have to do. For every job target, you may need a slightly different résumé: one that highlights one aspect of your work experience more than another. You may find it strategic at some point to prepare a résumé *for a particular company*. I've known candidates to prepare as many as a half-dozen different résumés, each tailored to a different kind of job.

Putting It Together

Now you're ready to put together your own résumé; but don't rush the process. You're going to need a few days. And when you've put together what you think is a good résumé, you should put it aside for a day or two, then come back to it for the finishing touches. It may take you as many as six different drafts to get it right. This doesn't mean that you're slow. Some of the world's best writers sometimes spend an entire day on a single paragraph. A good résumé is worth whatever time and effort it takes.

The Form

Résumés can take different forms, but I recommend the most familiar of them: the *chronological*. In this form, you list your work experience in reverse chronological order. The so-called *functional* form groups your experience according to specific categories, not according to time. Another form—known in some circles as the *hybrid*—combines the two. I'm not entirely sold on the functional form because some executives assume, when they see it, that you're trying to hide something (perhaps the fact that you've been out of a job for a long time).

Personal Data

Most résumé specialists suggest you list personal data at the top, near your name, address and phone number. It's certainly not an important feature, but as long as most readers of résumés expect to see it there, I recommend you put it on top. However, if you believe that some of that data can't help you, and might hurt you, insert it near the end. Keep this section very brief. Put down your birthdate and your marital status. Forget your spouse's name, mention your children's ages, but leave off their names, too. I've never understood why most résumés include information about health but virtually every résumé I've ever seen describes the health of the candidate as "excellent." So you might as well include it.

Education

The education section of the résumé should generally follow the personal data section. But if your education is not as adequate as you would like it to be for the job you're looking for, then show it after the experience section. If your résumé is two pages, make sure that your education appears on the second page. If your education is the highlight of your career, always insert it under personal data, but make sure there's enough room on the first page of the résumé for the most current job to be described.

Mention your higher education background only, and start with the highest level. Indicate the degree you earned, the subject you majored in, and the year you graduated. If you were an honor graduate or a Phi Beta Kappa or earned any similar distinction, mention it, but don't elaborate. If you have to describe an award in detail, it probably doesn't belong in your résumé. Any business-related training or special licenses should also go in this section, but skip the three-day seminars. And whatever you do, don't mention the fact that you've been to one of those human potential therapy courses. This section of your résumé should take up no more than five or six lines at the most.

How to Present Your Job Experience

The heart of your résumé is the section that capsulizes your work experience. It's the section most people who evaluate your résumé are going to look at first. It should take up about two thirds of the material in the résumé unless you're entry level or have very little related experience. Give this section more thought and more time than you give to any other.

A common fault in résumé writing is to belabor the obvious in the work experience section—usually at the expense of information that needs to be included. There is too much of

pure job description (often in jobs that require no such elaboration) and not enough information to dramatize how well
you performed the job. Here's an exaggerated example of
what I mean:

> PROFESSIONAL BASEBALL PLAYER. *Played shortstop. Fielded
> ground balls and threw to first base. Caught pop-ups and
> line drives. Accepted relay throws from outfield. Batted
> sixth in batting order. Duties included trying to get hits
> and drive in runs.*

Don't laugh. Most résumés I've seen commit the same sin to
one degree or another: from accountants whose blow-by-blow
description of what they did on a job was so specific I was surprised they didn't mention the make of the pen they used; from
magazine editors who would include in the comment of their
job phrases like "edited articles"; from a book designer whose
job description consisted of two words: "Designed books."
    Then what *do* you do when you go to describe a job?
Simple—you avoid the obvious and concentrate on the accomplishments. For instance:

> PROFESSIONAL BASEBALL PLAYER. *Starting shortstop for
> Phillies for nine seasons. Established league record with
> career fielding average of .978. Set team record for assists
> in 1978. Had three .300-plus seasons. Hit (in career) 178
> home runs. Final career average: .292.*

In this example, we're not only describing how you made
your living for the past nine years but giving detailed information that radiates accomplishment.
    Here is the true key to a "selling" résumé: presenting your
job experience not simply in terms of the mechanics of the
job but in terms of what you accomplished.

Cataloguing Accomplishments

Before you begin on the work experience section of your
résumé, you need to amass a catalogue of your career

accomplishments—assuming you haven't already done so. Remember, we're not looking here simply for your duties and responsibilities. We want *accomplishments*. If it's impossible for you to come up with accomplishments, you may have to rely solely on a straight description; but don't give up until you've tried the following exercise.

Write down on a separate sheet of paper or a file card each of the jobs you've held since you left school. Start with your most recent job. Write down at least five things you accomplished in that job (more if you can think of them). If you can't think of five, put down four, or three, but force yourself to think along these lines. Don't lie, but give yourself credit where credit is reasonably due. Don't worry about how it sounds as you write. Just get it down on paper. At this early stage in the résumé writing process, it's okay to use the first person. Here are some examples:

I developed a new training program for entry-level administrative employees, and as a result of it there was a noticeable drop in employee turnover.

I worked on and helped to administer a new training program for entry-level administrative employees. It was described by my supervisor as "the best program the company ever had."

Because of my knowledge of the restaurant business I was able to help the creative department develop a proposal that helped our firm gain a major restaurant chain as an account.

I was the editor who assigned and edited five different articles in 1979 that received awards from the Society of Magazine Writers.

If you're having trouble coming up with accomplishments, try completing the following incomplete statements:

I organized . . .
I created . . .
I established . . .
I revamped . . .
I developed . . .
I supervised . . .
I streamlined . . .
I strengthened . . .
I put into effect . . .
I helped to reduce . . .
I saved . . .
I improved . . .
I tied together . . .
Because of me the company . . .
Because of me the department . . .

You don't have to fill in all of these blanks. I offer them simply to get your mind moving in an accomplishment-oriented direction. As I mentioned earlier, leave out the first person in the résumé itself.

The Next Step

Once your job accomplishment sheets are filled out—and you should be as detailed at this stage as you can—you're ready to write the first draft of the job experience section.

Take your most recent job. Write down the position, the company name. If you think it's needed, explain what the company does.

For example:

Assistant Controller, ABC Electronics, Inc. A corporation manufacturing electronic components. Sales $20 million.

Next, in one *short* sentence, describe the scope and responsibility of your job:

Responsible for entire accounting function, including cost, budgets, statements, and systems.

Now go to the sheet of paper that lists this job. Choose what in your judgment are the four most important accomplishments, and put them in an abbreviated form.

Let's say your list reads, in part, as follows:

I established an effective system of job cost analysis, and as a result of it the company was able to change its product pricing and realize considerable profit.

You would write on your résumé draft:

Established system of job cost analysis that changed product pricing and improved profits.

Let's say one of the accomplishments read as follows:

I investigated potential acquisitions and, on the basis of these investigations, made recommendations as to purchase price. I once uncovered a major discrepancy in connection with a probable merger.

You might shorten this to:

Investigated potential acquisitions and recommended purchase price: uncovered merger-related discrepancy in 1978.

Keep these information fragments down to no more than ten words. Start with an active verb, and eliminate all nonessential words. Instead of:

I developed a new training program for entry-level administrative employees and as a result of it there was a noticeable drop in employee turnover . . .

Developed training program for entry-level administrative employees that cut employee turnover by 15 percent.

Following this procedure may be cumbersome to you at first, but stay with it. After you've done a few, the rest should come easier. Keep in mind what your objective is here: *to reflect as positive an image of yourself as possible.* The list of words on page 90 might help. Somehow, in some way, you must get across the contributions you have made to the companies you have worked for, and the accomplishments you can point to in each job you've held.

Depending upon how many jobs you've held, this portion of your résumé might run as long as a page or as short as a paragraph. Outside of keeping the whole résumé to no more than two pages, there are no rules here. If your list looks long, prune it. Don't detail your early jobs as much as your most recent ones. The fewer the jobs you list, the *more* accomplishments you should try to work in. The more jobs you list, the more selective you can be about the accomplishments.

Without cramping your style, I'd say that if your résumé indicates ten specific accomplishments, then you have a strong résumé.

Words to Create a Positive Impact

accelerated	generated	reduced
actively	guided	reinforced
adapted	improved	reorganized
administered	increased	responsible
approved	influenced	responsibilities
completed	implemented	revamped
conceived	interpreted	reviewed
conducted	launched	revised
conferred	led	scheduled
created	maintained	set up
delegated	participated	significantly
demonstrated	performed	simplified
developed	pinpointed	solved
directed	planned	strategy
effected	proficient at	streamlined
eliminated	programmed	strengthened
established	proposed	structured
expanded	provided	successfully
expedited	recommended	tied together
		triggered

Personal Comments

Most conventional résumé models do not include a place to make a personal comment about yourself, but I recommend you make just such a comment. Keep it brief (no more than three or four lines), but use the opportunity to say something nice about yourself. Be careful. It's one thing to toot your horn; it's another to give a Marine Band concert. This comment should be a conservative, but positive, assessment of what makes you special. Here's an example:

I'm self-motivated, well-organized, a hard worker, and in every job I've had, I've always been willing to make sacrifices to get results.

If you have trouble coming up with a comment you're comfortable with, some terms and phrases that might apply to you are given in the lists that follow.

For example, if you want to stress your competence, here are some words or phrases you might use:

creative	think and act maturely
strength in	comprehensive knowledge of
ability to	aggressive, tactful, and
cut out for	results-oriented
thoroughly trained	keep up with current
mastered	thorough understanding of
well grounded	capable of formulating and
proficient	directing
effective in	like to find a better way of
capacity for	doing things
adept at	not wedded to fixed ideas
technical competence in	integrity and drive
pre-plan everything	inspire confidence
know-how	like to make things happen
aptitude for	want to get involved
first hand knowledge of	ability to see the overall
practical approach to	picture
performance-oriented	ability to make practical
proven track record	decisions

If you want to stress your ability to handle details, try these:

detail-minded	methodical
pay attention to detail	careful
like detail	systematic
a stickler for detail	orderly
precise	excellent memory

accurate
well organized
get things done
perfectionist
take pride in work

fastidious
efficient
follow through
meet all due dates
adept with figures

These work well if you want to stress your ability to assume responsibility:

accelerated
alerted
automated
controlled
created
demonstrated
devised
established
expedited
fashioned
generated
initiated
installed
originated
sparked

streamlined
guided
revamped
coordinates
shape and direct
well versed in
heavily involved in
concentrated on
prime emphasis on
comprehensive
strong dedication to
solid foundation in
sound overview of
guided corporate policies

Words or phrases that indicate your desire to get ahead:

high-energy person
work day and night
thrive on hard work
find time to do everything
entrepreneurial viewpoint
enormous capacity to
meet deadlines
coolness under stress
perform well under pressure
self-motivated
steady persistence
make things happen

get things done on time
have lots of stamina
on the go constantly
compulsive drive
action-oriented
accept responsibility
tackle a job
energetic
vigorous
enthusiastic
a commitment to
troubleshooter

Words or phrases that reflect intelligence:

ability to think analytically	common sense
logical thinker	good memory
probing mind	creative
fast-thinking	ideas person
perceptive	mental capacity

Words or phrases that show you're profit-oriented:

profit-minded	drastically cut—without reducing sales
profit-conscious	
cost-oriented	tough on controls
expense-minded	knack for saving money
shortcut to	simplified procedures
streamlined	eliminated bottlenecks
efficient	set priorities
problem solver	initiated profitmaking plans
relieve paperwork jams	set up profit centers
ability to identify and solve problems	get quicker and more reliable information
results-oriented	across-the-board economy measures
reduce excessive costs	
strict control of	generated cost savings
controlled spiralling costs	ability to trim costs and increase efficiency
curtailed spending	

Words or phrases indicate management ability:

headed	people-handling skills
took charge	successful with people
administered	decision maker
authority over	command respect
closely supervised	ability to inspire others
directed	high-level supervisory skills
strong leader	leadership ability
spearheaded	developed subordinates
ranking member of	hard-driving doer
in charge of	willing to take the initiative

And words or phrases that are useful in an all-around sort of way:

self-disciplined	thrive in an environment
self-reliant	that . . .
self-confident	necessary ingredients for
conscientious	get along well with people
diplomatic	enjoy getting involved with
discreet	good back-up for . . .
tactful	good listener
persuasive	a need to excel
success-oriented	excellent work habits
competitive drive	keen sense of urgency
take nothing for granted	understand priorities
aptitude for	courage of convictions
mildly aggressive	professional attitude

Don't neglect these lists. You'll want to refer to them when you're sending out covering letters. And you can use them to give you some ideas on how to present yourself in job interviews.

Job Objectives

All things considered, you're better off *omitting* this section from your résumé, even though many job books suggest that you include it. I was never swayed one way or the other by what candidates wrote here; more often than not, it sounded forced and stiff. Some objectives, however, did make my Resumania file, among them:

I prefer informality like wearing sport shirt and sandals for footwear in the summer. I prefer setting my own pace. When things get slack, I like the right to walk out and get a haircut during working hours.

I want a position with a company where there is absolutely no drinking. I would consider performing civic activities where all expenses were paid by the employer.

The main problem with listing an objective is this: if the objective is too general, it doesn't mean anything; if it's too specific, it could limit your chances for jobs that don't fit the stated objective but nonetheless might be right for you. The only time I recommend putting an objective on your résumé is if you are tailoring the résumé for a specific company and a specific job. Otherwise, omit it.

Special Situations

Your background could reflect a problem of one kind or another that complicates the putting together of your résumé. There is no way of anticipating all the various problems that can crop up when you're writing a résumé, but here are some of the more common problem situations and the best way to respond to them.

If Your Personal Data Isn't Favorable

If you feel that your age—either being too young or too old—could hurt your chances, put it at the end of the résumé. Try to make your résumé longer than one page so that the "personal data" section doesn't appear on page one. Perhaps, by the time the résumé reader gets to your age, you'll have already earned yourself a closer look. The same holds true for marital status. Our surveys show that being divorced these days is no longer the obstacle it may have been years ago, but it could still pose a problem for you. You could, of course, omit any reference to your marital status and leave it at that; but the omission could serve to draw attention to it.

If You Didn't Finish College . . .

Not having graduated from college isn't as much of a problem once you've already been in the work force for five years or more, but it could be a strike against you if you're young. The only thing to do is put your education at the end. Also, expand on it by listing any business-related courses you might have taken.

If Your Record Includes Too Many Jobs . . .

One solution is to use the so-called functional résumé form in which you summarize your work experience in terms of job categories and not in the standard chronological order. A better approach is to highlight your present—or last job—and give it substantially more space than each of the others. If you have enough significant things to say about this last job, you could devote a separate category in the work experience section in which you summarize your responsibilities in the other jobs you've held.

If Your Last Job Isn't as Saleable as an Earlier One . . .

A common problem. There are a couple of ways to deal with it. One is to fudge somewhat the order in which you list jobs, tucking the dates into the body of the work experience section so they're not as noticeable. Another way is to list jobs in the proper order but give the most space to the job you feel is more saleable.

If You Have a One-Company Record . . .

No problem here at all. Simply show the name of the company on top of the experience section, and under it list a chronological history of your employment with that company, citing recent position first, and stressing accomplishment. In other words, handle it as if the jobs were with different companies.

If You Have a One-Industry Record . . .

This is only a problem if you are looking to *change* industries. One solution is to produce two résumés: One that mentions your industry and mentions the names of employers. The other that does not mention your industry, but includes dates and broad descriptions of the employers. Both, of course, detail your work experience.

Getting It Printed

Everything about your résumé is a reflection of you. This is why the résumé must not only read well but look as good as possible. Unless you are a professional typist with access to a typewriter with an attractive, businesslike typeface, don't type the résumé yourself. I consider myself a much better than average typist and I would never dream of typing the final draft of any résumé I wrote. Once you get it typed (and double—no, *triple* check it for mistakes), take it to a copy center and have it run off offset. Don't use one of those library copying machines that gives you poorly printed copies on oily paper. Have your résumé printed on bond paper of at least 60 lb. weight. You may have to go to a stationery store and deliver it yourself to the copy center, since most centers copy on cheaper grade papers. Stick to a standard 8½ by 11, and keep it simple. Some job counselors advise using a pastel shade or a textured linen kind of paper, but I much prefer a simple white, off-white or ivory heavy bond paper.

What You Should Do About References

First of all, leave them off the résumé. References are important, but not that important, and for a logical reason. Every interviewer knows that you're not going to refer your potential employer to anybody who isn't going to say nice things about you. Then again, you never know. I remember many years ago interviewing a young man for a job as office boy. The only reference he gave was his mother, so I called her. "Well," she said, "Jimmy will be a good boy once he gets a decent job." With a mother like that, you don't need enemies.

References are particularly important if you're getting fired. As long as you've maintained a reasonably decent relationship with your boss, you can still usually count on a reference letter from her or him (it may even help assuage the guilt of having to fire you). It's an accepted practice to draft such a letter yourself, then have the boss look it over. Some people might prefer to write their own references, so give your boss the option. In any case, never take a reference letter into an interview with you, and use any reference as sparingly as possible.

Résumé Samples—The Bad and the Good

Two résumés follow (pp. 95–98) describing an executive accountant. The first suffers from many of the problems common to poor résumés, yet I have seen hundreds with the same kinds of errors, typos, misspellings, construction, sequence and content. The second represents the way a résumé *should* read and look.

Let's review some of the problems on the first résumé:

• *General appearance.* The first résumé doesn't make you want to read it. It's too crowded and too wordy, and it is filled with errors.

• *First person.* Never put a "Mr." in front of your name on a résumé. Eliminate as much as possible the use of the first person "I."

• *"Objective."* My view is to eliminate it. It tends to be too limiting, producing fewer interviews. If you insist upon including objectives, make sure they are not too restrictive. One time objectives are useful is when you are pinpointing the résumé to one job at one firm.

• *Personal Data.* Far too much detail here. On a good résumé, this section rarely takes more than two lines. The candidate here should have left his Social Security number off, too.

• *Hobbies.* Too many, although I've seen three times as many on some résumés.

• *Memberships.* Everything's fine until the mention of memberships in the Admiral's Club and the Ambassador's Club. In case you are unfamiliar with them, one is owned by American Airlines, the other by TWA. They're used by frequent travelers. The only qualification for admission is the ability to pay the dues.

• *Education*. Stick to the highest level of education, unless the lower level offers a unique credential. Education should be shown in reverse chronological order, with the most recent first. This applicant is a college graduate—a fact buried in the middle of less important education. He also happens to be a CPA. I know this because of his memberships. This is not shown anywhere on the résumé. In my revision, I show it twice. Once on the top, after his name; and the second time on the line after his college education.

• *Experience*. It should be in *reverse* chronological order, the most recent job listed first. To simplify the résumé, and to concentrate on the most important facts, I left off his jobs while working his way through college. But if this person was entry level, or almost entry level, I would show employment while attending school.

Note in particular the lack of good solid information about his experience—the most important part of any résumé. This résumé doesn't show what the candidate *did* for these firms that would produce efficiency or profit. He also includes his salaries and reasons for termination—a mistake.

• *References*. Unnecessary for the résumé, since they would be made available at an interview for an interested hiring executive.

A Closing Thought on Résumés

A résumé that is doing what it's supposed to do will accomplish the following: (1) show that you contribute to whatever job you take; (2) show, implicitly, that you are organized, ambitious, and goal-directed; and (3) convey an overall image of you that says to the person reading the résumé you deserve a closer look. Your résumé will, or won't, do these things on the strength of how you present your work experience, on the tone and readability, and on its overall look.

I like to call a résumé that accomplishes all of these objectives a "positive" résumé. Many résumés I've come across have been positive in one area—contribution perhaps—but not in other areas. The most successful résumés, according to research our company conducted for over five years, are those that are positive on all three fronts. Take the time you need to stress your work experience within the framework of *accomplishment*. Take the time you need to put together your résumé in an organized and attractive format. Spend the extra money it takes to have it typed and presented in the most attractive manner possible.

Résumés *count*. They get you into the interview situation! And as I've been saying all along, in so many words, you can't hit a home run until you get up to the plate.

THE WRONG WAY

Mr. John J. Jones, 500 Second Ave., Oak Brook, Il, 222-1212

OBJECTIVE I am seeking a challenging position with a manufacturer in
the energy field in the Chicago area. I will consider relocating out-
of-town if the salary is at leas 35% above my present earnings plus a
car, stock options and other benefits...and a 5 year contract cancell-
able at my option. I will consider a position out of the energy field,
although I do not prefer it.

PERSONAL DATA I have been happily married to my wife Joan (ne: Brown).
She graduated from the University of Michigan in 1965 with a Batchelor's
degree in English. She teaches in the Oak Brook High School, and has
been their for three years. She was born on June 19, 1943. We have 2
adorable children: Marc Alan born on November 11, 1975 and Anne Eliz-
abeth born on September 19, 1977. In addition we have a two year old
poodle - Gigi. I am 42, born on April 7, 1940. I am 5' 11" tall and
weigh 165 pounds. My health is good. In fact, I have only been in the
hospital three times in my life. Once when I was born, the second time
I had a tonsillectomy of March 14, 1943 and a fractured tibia on February 2, 1978 as a result of a skiing accident. In the last 5 years I
have been home from work, as a result of the flu and a couple of bad
colds a total of 12 days.

I own my own home and a 1981 Chevrolet. I read the Chicago Tribune,
The Wall Stree Journal, Time, Newsweak and th Reader's Digenst.

My Social Security number is 111-03-0099.

HOBBIES AND INTERESTS Swimming, boating, fishing, skiing, bowling,
handbal, chess, bridge, woodworking and house painting. I enjoy spending time with my wife and children.

MEMBERSHIPS I am a member of the American Insitute of Certified Public
Accountants, the Illinois State Society of CPA's, the National Associ-
tion of Accountants, the Admiral's Club and the Ambassador's Club.

EDUCATION

1946 - 1954   Oak Brook Elementary School - Oak Brook, Illinois

1954 - 1959   Oak Brook High School - Oak Brook, Illinois

1959 - 1962   University of Illinois - Champagne, Illinois. Batchelor
              of Science degree awarded in Accounting.

1962   Dale Carnegie course in public speaking.

1967   Oak Brook High School - ADult Education - Woodworking.

1974   Oak Brook High School - Adult Education - Basic Computer
              Programming.

EXPERIENCE

1956 - 1959   Chicago Tribune. Sold newspapers.

1959 - 1962   Hamburger Happiness - Waiter. Worked my way through
              college.

1962 - 1964   Arthur Smith & Company. Certified Public Accountants.
              This is an international firm of accountants with 150
              offices and employes over 10,000 people. I served my
              internship with them doing routine accounting work.
              My salary at termination was $12,000 annually. I quit
              to go into private accounting.

1964 - 1978	Market Researchers Corporation. I started in Internal Audit and worked my way up to Assistant Controller. I left this job because the Controller was an incompetent, and it looked as though he would never be terminated. Salary $19,450.
1978 - to date	Widget Corp. of America. This company is a division of Widget International, Inc. I was hired to head up their Internal Audit Department, and was later promoted to become Assistant Controller, and when the Controller left the company I was appointed to his job. I plan on leaving the company because of personal differences with the President. Salary with bonus $31,600.
REFERENCES	Judge William Green - 200 Main St. - Oak Brook, Il
	Mayor Thomas White - 100 Fourth St. - Oak Brook, Il
	James Blue, President - Market Researchers Corp.
	Mary White, Partner - Arthur Smith & Co.

THE RIGHT WAY

JOHN J. JONES, CPA
500 Second Avenue
Oak Brook, IL 60521
(312) 222-1212

PERSONAL

Birth Date: April 7, 1940   Married, 2 children
Height: 5' 11" Weight: 165 lbs.   Health: Excellent

EDUCATION

BS - Accounting - 1962 - University of Illinois - Dean's List
Certified Public Accountant - Illinois - 1965

EXPERIENCE

1978 - Present

WIDGET CORPORATION OF AMERICA
Division of Widget International, Inc.
Largest manufacturer of micro-widgets in the world.

Controller

Responsibilities include financial reporting, determining applicable accounting standards to insure maximum internal
control. Prepare capital expenditure reports for parent
company. Supervise internal auditing, cost and tax departments. Conduct special studies in connection with acquisitions. In complete charge of budgets and cash flow. Li-
aison with computer department. Have a good knowledge
of the Systems 34.

The controller's department has been operating at the same
cost as it did 4 years ago even though sales increased 62%.
This has been brought up at every executive committee meeting as an example of good management.

1964 - 1978

MARKET RESEARCHERS, INC.
Multi-branch research for large advertisers and ad agencies.

Assistant Controller

Established an Internal Audit Department which was so effective that we uncovered a fraud that was operating for
2 years. This resulted in a promotion to assistant controller.

Assisted in the development and implementation of a Systems
3 computer for accounts receivable, payable and payroll.
The system produced a detailed sales analysis that encouraged management to expand its most profitable services.

EXPERIENCE
(Continued)

1962 - 1964   ARTHUR SMITH & CO.
                     Certified Public Accountants - One of the largest in the U.S.

                     Senior Accountant

                     Audited and reviewed financial statements of 21 different
                     company clients in various industries. Electronics manu-
                     facturing, book publishing, insurance, transportation and
                     energy corporations. Reviewed taxes and evaluated in-
                     ternal controls, accounting systems, SEC and stockholder's
                     reports.

                     Recommended improvements in audit procedures which en-
                     abled us to produce a more useful and comprehensive audit
                     without increasing audit time.

PROFESSIONAL   American Institute of Certified Public Accountants
AFFILIATIONS   Illinois State Society of CPAs
                     National Association of Accountants
                     Beta Gamma Sigma Honor Society

OTHER INTERESTS   Swimming, skiing, chess and bridge.

COMMENTS   I enjoy a challenge and quickly adapt to new projects.
                     I am proud of my ability to get things done, and I get
                     along very well with my colleagues. I am willing to re-
                     locate out-of-town.

V

Knocking on the Right Doors

A lead leads to a lead.

For most job hunters, opportunity rarely knocks even *once*. *You* have to do the knocking, the digging, the searching. *You* have to develop your own leads and figure out the best way to follow them up. And you can't rely on the conventional route—the ads that appear in the newspapers. The conventional route in job hunting is crowded with other job hunters. The odds are long and the going is slow.

In this chapter, we're going to look at how you go about generating interviews for yourself. I'm going to emphasize the importance of being *active*. One of the worst mistakes you can make in a job search is to stop moving forward: to sit back and wait for job leads to materialize, for agencies and recruiters to call, for want ads that appeal to you to appear in the newspapers. If you do, you will spend 90 percent of your job search time doing just that—waiting.

Setting Up a Job Strategy

Job leads can originate almost anywhere—from dozens of sources. But the sources, of course, will differ in terms of both the number of leads they generate and the quality of those leads.

You should set up your strategy accordingly. The classified section of your Sunday newspaper, for instance, is a generally fruitful source of job leads. You could read about as many as six different openings in fifteen minutes. But newspaper advertisements get read by just about everybody looking for work. You're operating in a crowded field, and it won't be easy to get yourself singled out. On the other hand, an introduction to a certain person in a certain company with a job opening for which it hasn't yet begun to advertise could sometimes take days, but will give you a *direct* shot at the job.

So, keeping these two variables in mind—the *number* of job possibilities a source can generate and the *quality* of those leads—you can give your campaign a degree of efficiency that will be lacking in most. Think of yourself as being on a treasure hunt. Hidden within a confined area and in different places are a dozen or so items of varying value. The less valuable items are nearby, easy to locate. The more valuable items are tougher to find; you have to dig deeper. If you're smart, you don't spend all of your time looking for the less valuable items simply because they're easy to find. Nor do you ignore the relatively easy items in an all-out effort to find the more valuable item. You strike a balance.

What I'm going to do in this chapter is describe in detail the most common sources of job leads and how best to pursue them. Some of them—want ads, for instance—are relatively easy to pursue but may yield leads of limited value. Others— good personal contacts, for instance—are tougher to pursue but, in many cases, well worth the extra time it takes to pursue them. All the leads, however, are *worth* pursuing. You have to set up a plan that strikes the most effective balance.

Contacts: Pyramiding the Name Game

Personal contacts are, hands down, your best source of job leads. Seek them out, pursue them, and use them intelligently.

By "personal contacts," I'm talking about anybody you know, or can get to, who can do any of the following:

1. Offer you a job.

2. Refer you to someone who can offer you a job.

3. Refer you to somebody who can arrange an interview or read your résumé.

4. Tell you of a job opening.

5. Give you the name of somebody who can do any of the above.

6. Give you the name of somebody who can give you the name of someone else who can do any of the above. There is no limit.

Everybody—yes, everybody—has these kinds of contacts, which is to say that everybody knows somebody, or knows somebody who knows somebody, who might produce a job lead, or who might give useful information or provide an introduction to a person who can facilitate your job search. Not everybody, though, utilizes his contacts to maximum advantage. I've worked with candidates who were reluctant to seek the help of even close relatives. Why? In most cases, it was nothing more than a matter of pride. As many candidates put it: "I want to get this job *on my own*."

These are noble sentiments, but the fact is that many job candidates who get good jobs get outside help at some point along the way. Maybe it's a phone call from a business associate with a tip on an opening. Or a personal introduction to a would-be employer. Maybe it's nothing more than a personal recommendation. But it's *something*—and it's frequently the something that can tilt the odds toward that particular candidate.

Setting Up Your Own Contact List

Anybody you know who might conceivably be of help to you in your job search should be considered a "contact." How much this person can help you isn't easy to predict. Nor can you know, until you've asked, how far a contact will go when the time comes to pull strings or go to bat for you. One of the most dispiriting experiences in job hunting is to discover that a person you always thought you could count on is suddenly difficult to reach now that you're looking for work. Recently I heard about a man who was working as a correspondent in Los Angeles for a national news magazine. He became friendly, as the result of the assignment, with the head person at one of the major studios. They socialized, played tennis together. The studio man would constantly tell the correspondent that he was wasting his time on the magazine and should come to work at the studio.

Well, the time came when the magazine wanted to reassign the writer, but the writer didn't want to leave the West Coast. So he quit his job, figuring that with his contact at the major studio, he'd be better off than he was before. There was only one problem. Once the correspondent no longer worked for the magazine, the studio executive was suddenly hard to find. The correspondent never even got as far as an interview, and was out of work for six months before he got another job.

Your primary pool of contacts is the people you're the closest to, your relatives and close friends. Go there first. It's not asking for charity when you ask a relative or friend to set up an introduction for you, or to give you some names of people: *you're simply using the most obvious source for the information and the help you need.* Wouldn't you do the same for them?

A phone call gets the job done. Don't be evasive. Don't figure that if you let people know you need help, somebody will *volunteer* this help. Who knows, some people might worry that offering you help could injure your feelings. Worse, being evasive might create the impression that you're fishing around for a loan.

So be as specific as you can. Know ahead of time *who* the person you're asking for help might introduce you to, or how, specifically, that person might be of help. People tend to respond much more readily to specific requests ("Frank, could you get me an introduction to the marketing head of Widgets, Inc.?") than to general requests ("Frank, do you know anybody who's looking for a marketing supervisor?")

Being direct and specific actually takes pressure off the contact you're approaching. The person no longer has to search his or her own mind or conscience for ways to help you. You're not handing over the whole responsibility of finding you a job: you're asking for a specific favor—a favor that, presumably, is not terribly difficult to perform.

If close friends or relatives are not in an obvious position to help you, let them know what your situation is and the kind of thing you're looking for. Ask, simply, that they keep their ears open for you.

Second-Level Contacts

You don't stop pursuing personal contacts once you've gone through the handful of friends and relatives with whom you're not embarrassed to discuss your situation. There is usually a huge group of second-level contacts who could prove equally valuable, *if* you approach them in the right way. I include in this category the following:

1. Your business colleagues, past and present.

2. Former bosses.

3. Former subordinates, who presumably have moved up the ladder.

4. Your college professors.

5. Your company's bank or your bank.

6. Lawyers, ad agencies, buyers, salespersons—anyone who gets around.

7. School alumni.

8. Members of a club or religious organization.

9. The professional people you deal with in your personal life—doctors, dentists, etc.

10. Trade organization or professional society leaders.

11. Your banker or stockbroker.

Early in your job search, set aside several hours and write down as many names as you can under each of these categories. Decide how each person might help you. If the person is in a position to help you *directly,* put a check after the name and contact him or her first. But don't ignore the rest. They could arrange introductions, or you might use them as sounding boards.

Here again, don't beat around the bush when you call them. Be as specific as possible. And before you get in touch with a contact, *make sure you have already formulated in your mind the role this person can have in your job search.*

Generating Your Own Contacts

Everybody you meet in the course of your job search is not only a potential contact but a lead to a contact. One especially fertile and often overlooked source of names is the person who interviews you for a job you don't get. Even if you don't get hired, you can sometimes emerge from such an interview with a couple of names of people who might be of help. How do you get the names? The simplest and most direct way: you ask for them ("Can you think of anybody it might be useful for me to talk to?"). When you get the names, find out if it's okay to use the name of the person who recommended them. Be positive ("It's okay if I use your name, isn't it?").

Keep a small notebook with you at all times and become a name scavenger. The more names you collect, the better your chances of connecting. Maybe the person whose name you've been given can't help but knows somebody who can. Maybe it will take you a succession of four or five contacts before you finally get someone who can be of direct help.

There is no such thing as having *too many* names of people to contact. The most each name costs you is the minute or two it takes you to phone them. You might call twenty-five people without getting anything that takes you closer to a good job, but the twenty-sixth call could put you on the scent of one. So keep calling. If you've been enterprising in getting up a contact list, you may have as many as one hundred or more names, so set up a timetable. Set aside at least an hour a day for making phone calls. Call at least ten people a day. Try to elicit an additional name or two from each person you talk to. *Play the name game to the hilt.*

Keep a record of every name, along with the name of the person who gave you the reference. That person may be as important as the name itself when the time comes to make contact. That person's name is the "in." It gets you past the secretary, to the person you want to speak to ("Hello, Mr. Fields? My name is Mary Jones. I'm a friend of . . ."). This is the standard opening. Don't vary it too much. Occasionally, you may find that the person isn't familiar with the contact. This could mean that your contact has been exaggerating his or her relationship with the employer. It may not even matter. The executive might talk with you anyway.

I repeat, don't worry if you're finding that most of your phone calls are "a waste of time." Expect it. Most of the calls you make *will* be a waste of time, but the next call you make may not be.

The only thing to be careful of is people who are too embarrassed or too vain to tell you they can't help and "invent" situations the better to keep your morale up. I've heard of job candidates who've wasted three or four days tracking down a lead that originated from a friend who was well meaning but didn't represent a situation the way it really was.

And don't underestimate the value of what I call the "courtesy" interview. A "courtesy" interview is one in which the person granting the interview has no desire at all to see the candidate but is doing it as a favor to the candidate's friend. True, there may not be a job, but you can sometimes impress an interviewer in one of these situations so that a genuine opportunity opens up.

Something else. Don't expect too much from introductions to the top people in the companies you're pursuing. As a general rule, the higher up a person is in an organization, the more that person is in a position to help. But very often the most a top executive is going to do for you is to shake hands, make some small talk, and then shuttle you off to personnel. If you have any say in the matter, try to connect with the person who heads the specific department you'll be working for if you get hired. In certain situations, being "recommended" by the president of a company could actually work *against* your chances. The person doing the hiring may resent the interference. But take the interview from whomever is available.

Want Ads

The most obvious and easily tapped of all job lead sources is the help-wanted section of your local newspaper. But what's obvious in job hunting isn't always productive or efficient. To build a job hunt campaign solely, or even largely, around help-wanted ads is to follow the foolish example of the man in the old joke who loses his wallet on the corner of Main Street and Fifth, but goes looking for it on the corner of Main Street and Fourth. Why? Because there's more light at Main Street and Fourth.

Here is one thing to bear in mind about want ads: *the majority of job openings never get advertised in the newspaper.* So, if want ads are the only job source you're tapping, you're closing yourself off from a big chunk of the job market—as much as 75 percent, according to most surveys. Secondly, once an advertisement for a good job appears in the want ads, the competition for that job automatically heats up. Some ads in a major metropolitan newspaper draw as many as five hundred replies.

Follow the want ads closely, but don't allow them to dominate your job hunt campaign. Keep in mind that want ads reveal to you only a small slice of the job market, and accept the fact that when you respond to an ad, regardless of how qualified you are, you're playing a numbers game, with the odds against you. To pursue this avenue of job searching effectively, you play the game, but keep in mind the odds.

Sources of Want Ads

The chief source of want ads in most cities is the classified section of the local Sunday paper, but don't confine your search to the local Sunday paper alone. Papers in nearby cities or cities you may relocate to are important, too. Trade or professional magazines in your particular field are likely to list positions available. *The Wall Street Journal* is a good source of want ads, even though many of the jobs offered may require relocation. The Sunday classified and business sections of the largest metropolitan newspapers, particularly the *New York Times* and the Los Angeles *Times,* are thick with advertisements for job openings not necessarily confined to their own metropolitan areas. (The problem, though, is that some large metropolitan papers—the *New York Times* being one of them—do not distribute the Sunday classified to areas outside their immediate metropolitan region. You may have to find somebody with access to these newspapers to send you the sections each week, or else contact the newspaper directly to find out how to get a copy sent to you.)

Don't ignore local papers in suburban areas, even though these papers tend to advertise lower-level jobs. Get friends who receive newspapers you don't to send the want ad sections to you.

Going Through the Ads

Be systematic when you're looking for job leads in the classified sections of newspapers and magazines. At the outset of your campaign, you should go through the want ad section from A to Z, as if you were reading a good novel.

Get the sense early on of the different headings under which job leads of interest to you may appear. There is no uniform system governing which jobs fall under which headlines. Depending on who has placed the ad, a typical executive position could well appear under any of a half-dozen headlines. Most newspapers list help-wanted advertising alphabetically, by job title. If a company places an ad for an assistant controller, it will probably be classified under the letter A. Yet most assistant controllers will look under the letter C for controller. This means that if you answer that ad, the competition will be reduced and your opportunity the greater. Sometimes a newspaper misclassifies an ad; the result is almost no response. In that event, the paper would probably give the advertiser a free run, but it gives you a head start.

Occasionally, too, a company inadvertently misleads the reader. A job described as administrative supervisor, for instance, may be, in fact, a standard secretarial position. Sometimes, too, the title is so vague it's impossible to tell what the job entails.

An assistant to the president, for instance, may call for a person who is sales-oriented, or factory-oriented, or financially-oriented. The lesson: don't base decisions purely on job titles.

Your system should allow you to keep track of all the ads you respond to. Use a felt-tip marker or highlighter to mark those ads that loom as worthy of response. Once you've gone through a publication, cut out the ads you want and paste each one on a 5 by 8 file card. (Make sure you don't cut out an ad that backs up to the one you are clipping out. In such a case, type one of them on the card.) Mark on the card the publication and the date the ad appeared. This will accomplish two things: one, you won't lose track of ads should the newspaper or magazine be thrown out inadvertently; two, you'll never run the risk of mentioning an incorrect date or the wrong publication with your response.

Use each of these file cards as a "log" for the job pasted to it. Note the date of your response. In the event you get an interview, the ad will be a good starting point for your interview preparation.

Develop a routine. Set aside a certain period two or three times a week to be devoted exclusively to the want ad phase of your job search. As a general rule, you should answer ads within a week after they appeared. But if you see an ad for which you consider yourself the ideal candidate and you detect a sense of urgency in the wording, answer it immediately—perhaps with a telegram or Mailgram.

On the other hand, you should keep in mind that most companies figure on anywhere from six weeks to three or four months to fill a job of substance. So the bigger and more important a job is, the longer many companies tend to look. *Because an ad that appeared five weeks ago hasn't appeared again doesn't mean the job has been filled*. It simply means the company has stopped advertising for candidates. If you're smart, in fact, you'll go through the want ads of papers five and six weeks old for leads.

Keep a record on your card of all correspondence received from the employer. Note whether the response was a form letter from the personnel department or a personal letter from one of the company's executives. You'll be keeping these letters on file anyway, of course, but having a record on 5×8 cards of each job opening you apply to gives you an efficient means of keeping track of the leads that look more promising.

Which Ads to Respond To

Answering want ads is a numbers game, so the general rule is to respond to any advertisement that sounds interesting, albeit with certain caveats.

If you're currently working, tread carefully where blind ads are concerned. Why? Well, as I explained in chapter I, you don't know who is getting the response, and you have no idea what they'll do with it. Maybe the person on whose desk the letter eventually lands is a personal friend of your boss. How do you know that as a favor to the friend, your boss may not report that a top employee (you) is getting itchy? It's a small world.

And how do you know that the letter you send in response to a blind ad won't end up on your boss's desk? Don't laugh. I've been told of some employers routinely running blind ads the better to see which of their employees are looking for new jobs. Some of these companies are careful to hide their true identity; they'll even present themselves in the ad as being in a different industry or a different location.

Some of what I've just said may strike you as slightly paranoid, but I don't think I'm exaggerating the dangers.

Under the best of circumstances, the odds of your actually ending up with the job you read about in a blind ad are very long. Compared to the ever-present possibility that an answer to a blind ad could very well cost you your present job, they are not worth the gamble. The blind ad is an invitation to unemployment.

Avoiding the "Qualifications" Trap

Don't let the "qualifications" listed in the ad overintimidate you. Many companies list certain qualifications merely to keep to a reasonable number the volume of responses. Don't let words like "desirable," "preferable," and "knowledgeable" keep you from responding. If an ad states "a minimum of three years experience" in a field but you only have a year or so, respond anyway. Just make sure that the letter which accompanies your résumé makes a convincing case as to why you should be considered. Point out where you do not conform, and quickly add some of your outstanding strengths.

Similarly, if the listed salary is somewhat below the minimum you've set for yourself but the job sounds like something you'd like, respond. Who knows, if you get an interview and impress the person you talk to enough, you might even get the salary raised. And if the job isn't exactly what you're looking for but the company sounds interesting, again, respond. It's a foot in the door. You'll never know all about a job until you've had an interview.

Personnel Agencies and Recruiters

Getting jobs for people is a big industry, and the specialists in the industry describe themselves in different ways. There are personnel agencies, personnel recruiters, executive recruiters, executive search firms, placement services, and so on. Deciding whom to approach for help can be confusing, to say the least.

Let me do my best to clarify the situation for you. Practically speaking, there is almost no difference between a personnel agency and a company that describes what it does as "recruiting," "searching," "placing," or anything similar. Everybody is doing basically the same thing: getting job openings from companies and looking for candidates to send on interviews. In certain instances, a company looking to fill a specialized or very high level job will pay a placement firm an advance fee; but usually the fee in a placement situation gets paid (by the company getting the new candidate) once the job has been filled.

The chief difference between recruiters (also known as "head-hunters") and agencies is that the recruiters, on the average, confine their attention to jobs in the higher salary ranges. Recruiters are more likely than personnel agencies to have jobs in the $100,000 a year range. On the other hand, recruiters are less likely to *specialize* in a particular occupation or industry than personnel agencies, which is why they will generally charge a client company a higher fee. Each new assignment obliges them to start their search from the beginning.

There are, of course, exceptions: recruiters who specialize in a particular field. And, all things being equal, you should go to someone—be it a personnel agency or a recruiter—who specializes in your particular occupation or industry. This isn't to say ignore an opening simply because it doesn't originate from a firm that specializes; never ignore *any* lead. But you'll do better, all in all, by concentrating your attention on the firms who know your field.

Knowing Which to Choose

Like any profession, the placement business has its good apples and its bad apples. In the better companies, you'll find men and women who are well connected to the various fields they work in, who have experience, and who have earned the confidence and respect of the people to whom they send candidates for interviews. These companies won't waste your time. They won't pressure you into jobs you shouldn't be taking.

The not-so-good recruiters and agencies are staffed with high-pressure salespeople who may not understand the personnel business, who may have no special experience in it, and who have little regard for either the companies they work with or the candidates they seek to attract.

Being able to differentiate the good from the not so good isn't as difficult as you might think. It's a matter of keeping your eyes open and trusting your instincts.

To begin with, the better recruiters and agencies didn't go into business yesterday. They've usually been around for a few years. They have established reputations. They're not plagued by constant employee turnover themselves.

Secondly, the better recruiters and agencies, as I've already mentioned, often specialize in one particular field or fields, be it advertising, the service industry, computers, financial, sales, or whatever. It's easy to find out which agencies and recruiters specialize in your particular field. Read the want ads to see which ones are advertising the most positions in your field. Ask business friends which agency or recruiter *they* would suggest.

Once you get a lead on one or several that look as if they can help you, it's up to you—your judgment and your instincts—to decide whether working with them is in your best interests. You can usually tell after your first interview with a placement person (if you're working with a recruiter) or an agency whether it's in your best interest to work with them. You will want to deal with people who are pleasant and reassuring but also businesslike. You deserve to be treated with respect, but be wary of anybody who seems *overly* complimentary, who *guarantees* that you've come to the right place, and who goes out of his or her way to convince you not to go anywhere else.

Trust your judgment. If you find one or two agencies or recruiters who appear to know the field you're interested in and you feel comfortable with them, there may not be a need to spread yourself any thinner. Limiting your search to one or two firms is an especially good idea if you're currently employed.

Still, there is nothing to prevent you from contacting as many agencies and recruiters as you want. Working with several agencies or recruiters instead of one or two may complicate your job search somewhat, but it also increases your chances for agency-generated job leads. If you're looking in more than one city, you have little choice but to use services in each city unless they have multiple offices.

Getting the Most out of Agencies and Recruiters

Be honest and reasonable with agencies and recruiters, but keep your self-interest in mind, and don't let yourself be pressured into making decisions that don't serve your best interests. Some agencies or recruiters may ask for an "exclusive" on your search. If you're convinced that they are reputable, and your situation isn't desperate, consider it, but only for a limited period of time. Otherwise, keep your options open.

If you're working with more than one agency, you might run into the problem of overlap: two agencies offering you the same position. Should an agency or recruiter talk to you about a job you've previously discussed with somebody else (or a job that sounds like one you've previously discussed) here's what to do: inform them that you've already been spoken to about that job. An ethical agency or recruiter in this situation will back off politely. An unethical one will try to work it out so that that placement fee will be all theirs—or else create enough of a fuss that the client will either pay two fees or split the fee between the two services. If you sense pressure from the second recruiter, hold your ground and defend the first one. Then tell the first agency or recruiter what has happened and don't deal with the second one again.

Obviously, no agency or recruiter can do a good job for you if you don't cooperate, or if you are not able to communicate to them your qualifications, skills, and goals. Your initial interview is very important. Be cooperative and honest. Get some feedback from the person you're meeting with. Make sure the two of you are on the same track, and that the placement person knows what you're looking for.

You don't necessarily have to be the best of friends, but you should respect the judgment of the person who's handling your search. If there's a personality clash, see about having somebody else in the firm handle your situation. In all of your dealings with an agency or recruiter, be courteous and reasonable. Being difficult and demanding won't help your cause at all. Theoretically, agency personnel and executive recruiters have to divorce their personal feelings about a client from the client's job qualifications. But if *you* were a recruiter or somebody working for a personnel agency, and you had two similarly qualified job candidates, one of them pleasant and cooperative, the other a constant bother, who would you offer the opening to first?

The Forms You Should and Shouldn't Sign

Most agencies and recruiters will ask you to sign certain forms. Some of these are in your interests to sign, others are not. One form you may be asked to sign gives the agency or recruiter the right to check your references. Without your signature, agencies and recruiters are forbidden by federal law to check out references. Refusing to sign this form will cut down on the opportunities you'll have a chance to explore. If you're currently employed and your employer doesn't know you're looking, you should sign this form with the understanding that no current references can be checked at this time. As far as standard application forms go, fill them out as completely as possible, even if the information is covered in a résumé. And it's not a bad idea to have a "dummy" application with you when you visit agencies, so you don't have to spend extra time looking up numbers or addresses, or trying to remember dates.

References can be a touchy matter, particularly if you're conducting a job search without the knowledge of your current employer. But don't take too rigid a position. As good as you are, as reliable and as competent as you are, you will arouse suspicion if you list references but prevent an agency or recruiter from checking on them.

Forms regarding fees are a different matter. Most agencies and recruiters these days get all of their fees from the company once they've placed a candidate. But a few might ask you to sign a contract that would make you responsible for the fee in the event you accept a job and then later change your mind, or in the event you join the company and quit a month or two later. I'm not saying you should never sign any forms relating to the payment of a fee. Just make sure you read the form first and understand exactly what you're signing.

One final word. *No recruiter or agency has the right to know where else you have been interviewed before coming to them, so there's no need to tell them.* Some will ask you this question routinely and tell you that by letting them know where you've already been, you're helping them to prevent overlap. You could also be told that most of the companies in their field are their clients and that the agency or recruiter doesn't want to cover ground that's already been covered.

That's what you're *told.* The trouble is that most agencies and recruiters ask these kinds of questions for no other reason than to get a line on jobs so that they can send out other candidates. So why increase the competition?

Employment Career Counselors

Watch your step here. Undoubtedly, there are experienced employment counseling specialists (many of them with degrees in psychology and counseling) who can enable you to clarify your career goals, understand your own potential better, and perhaps help you put together a résumé. My personal feeling is that most people are able to do these things for themselves, but this is not to say that these counselors can't be of help in some instances.

The companies you should be wary of are the ones that ask you for an upfront fee of as much as $8,000, for which they promise not only to put together a winning résumé and to give guidance, but imply that they'll virtually "place" you. Don't bet on it. Investigations into many of these firms show that the exclusive "leads" you get are no more than names from a list that you could get by yourself for a good deal less money. As a general rule, you should be wary of any employment service that charges an upfront fee. Be particularly suspicious if they promise you the moon.

Job Leads by Mail

A strong letter, written to the right person, is an extremely effective way of creating your own job leads. Some people argue that next to having a direct personal contact to someone in a hiring capacity, a letter (assuming it does its job) offers you your best chance of getting into the interview situation. *Our Burke survey showed that nearly 100 percent of unsolicited letters to top management are read, and that 80 percent produce some sort of response,* even though the response, in many cases, is nothing more than an acknowledgment that your letter was received.

The beauty of a letter is that it goes *directly* to the person with the power to hire you. It thus bypasses some of the people who have the power to say no. I've been saying all along that a key to successful job hunting is keeping to a minimum the number of people who can say no to you. No other approach except a personal introduction can do this. You can't simply pick up the phone and arrange for an interview with the person who has the power to hire you. You probably wouldn't get by the secretary. Even if you did, the executive you get to is likely to resent the intrusion. A letter gives you a chance to present your story the way you want it presented. Never underestimate the power of a letter. It is an approach to which most executives are reasonably receptive. Not every letter you send is going to produce the response you're looking for, but you can be fairly certain that the letter will be *read*. That's more than can be said for résumés sent in response to want ads.

Strategic Approaches to Letter Writing

Mounting a solid letter-writing campaign takes time and effort and, in some cases, sizeable expense. But I'm convinced that the time, the effort, and the expense are more than worth it.

There are different types of letters. The most effective generally are directed to a specific individual in a particular company. I call these "customized letters." They are directly keyed to a person in a company, to a problem the company is facing, or to some change in that individual's role in the company. You might write such a letter in response to a statement the individual has made that's been printed in a magazine or newspaper, or a speech you heard at an association meeting. You might write such a letter in response to a promotion announcement you read about in a newspaper or trade magazine.

Your letter should use the statement or the promotion announcement as a springboard to present your story—what you think you can offer and why you think it is in the best interests of this individual to arrange an interview with you. The only problem with this kind of letter is time: the time you spend writing that letter is time invested in that job situation alone. So, unless you're prepared to spend several hours a day writing letters, you're not going to be able to send out more than a half-dozen letters a week.

A second type of letter is generally known as the "broadcast letter," but I prefer to call it an "action letter." This is sent to an individual at a particular company, but the content never changes. The advantage of this type of letter is that once you've written it, you can send it out in large quantities, as long as you're willing to incur the mailing expense. There are ways of preparing these so that each has the appearance of being written specifically for an individual, but most executives can nonetheless tell the difference between a truly personal letter and an action letter that's going out to a lot of other people. Some executives won't hold this against you, if your letter presents a compelling enough case; but there's no question that this isn't as strong or strategic an approach as the first letter.

A third type of letter—and one you don't hear much about—combines elements of the action letter and the individualized letter. Let's call this the "customized action letter." The bulk of the letter (the part that describes your qualifications) is the same in all of the letters you send. But you personalize this letter with an opening paragraph—and perhaps a closing paragraph—that is keyed to the person you're writing. This is a little more expensive and a little more time-consuming than a straight action letter, but less expensive and time-consuming than an individualized letter.

Making Your Letters Look Professional

In order to launch a letter-writing campaign of any consequence, you're going to need professional assistance. An individualized letter, of course, has to be typed on an individual basis, but your action and customized letters can be mechanically reproduced, in a way that will let you add the address and salutation without making it appear that these have been tacked on. Standard photocopying, ditto process, or photo offset will *not* accomplish this. You may match up the typeface, but the shading is likely to differ. Word processors are probably the best means at present of giving an individualized appearance to mechanically reproduced letters. Consult a copying specialist before making any final decisions.

The main thing to remember here is that having letters reproduced in a way that *looks* professional and doesn't have the obvious appearance of boiler-plate may be more expensive than photocopy, but if you can afford it, it's worth the extra money.

Making a Persuasive Case

Whichever form of letter you use in a direct mail campaign, the basic purpose of the letter remains the same: *you want the letter to lead to an interview*.

Based on the figures I cited above from our Burke study, you can expect 80 percent of your letters to produce a response. Other studies suggest that while most of these responses will be polite refusals, anywhere from 2 to 10 percent of your letters should take you a step further in your quest. Naturally, the better and more persuasive the letter, the better your chances of getting this kind of favorable response.

A good action letter should do what a good résumé does: it should present a convincing case on your behalf. It should say to the person reading this letter that you're someone who is worth seeing. Your ability to get this message across will depend not only on the information contained in the letter but on the way the letter is written—particularly its tone. There are definite skills involved in writing a good letter. I'll point out what I consider to be the most important features of the kinds of letters we're talking about, and then talk briefly about how to write an effective letter.

1. *Be direct and to the point*. Your letter is the vehicle by which you hope to get an interview. It should arouse the interest of the reader, not tell the story of your life or present a detailed explanation of your philosophies or views. Keep the letter to no more than two pages, but don't let it be so brief that it doesn't make a convincing case in your behalf.

2. *Stress accomplishments, not experience*. In the same way that a good résumé should stress what you've accomplished, not just what jobs you've held, a letter should do more than simply describe your experience. Assume that there are any number of candidates who, on paper, look as good as you do. Your job in this letter is to single yourself out. You do this by describing specific, tangible accomplishments.

3. *Don't oversell yourself*. As good as you think you are, don't make the mistake of tooting your horn too loudly in the letter. Statements like: "You'll be making a terrible mistake if you don't set up an interview for me as soon as possible" will usually scare off most managers. Let your accomplishments make their own point. It shouldn't be necessary for you to come out and say how good you are. The facts should speak for themselves.

4. *Make absolutely sure you have the company's name, the executive's name, and the executive's position correct*. Check and double check. Is it The Evans Company, Evans Company, Evans Company, Inc., or The Evans Corporation? Is the executive you're writing to the Director of Marketing, the Director of the Marketing Division, or the Marketing Division Director? Don't take any chances misplacing a letter or a comma. (The first thing I often noticed when I received action letters was a misphrasing of the company name, and it

always made me less receptive to the content of the letter. It looked as if the letter was hastily done.)

If you don't know the name of an executive you want to contact, there's an easy enough way to find out: call the company. Simply say that you have a letter you want to send to the director of sales (or whatever position), and could somebody give the spelling of the person's name and the exact title.

Writing an Effective Letter

You don't have to be Hemingway or F. Scott Fitzgerald to write letters that can produce job leads. It's a matter of knowing what to say and saying it in as simple and direct a way as possible. You may have your own style of writing letters, but what follows is a general guide that should work well in most situations.

The Opening. Your opening paragraph should tell the person reading the letter why it is worth his or her time to read on. Your purpose in this first paragraph is to make some *connection* to the person reading the letter. Any time you can use a familiar name as an introduction, do so. For example:

```
I am writing you at the suggestion of a mu-
tual friend, Roger Phillips, who felt that
it might be to our advantage to meet.
```

Do your best to intrigue the person immediately:

```
Some people might think it's a bad time to
be looking for a position in the automotive
industry, but I have some ideas that might
interest you and I'd love the chance to talk
them over with you.
```

Everybody who gives a statement likes to know that that statement was read. It's a perfect opening for a job candidate writing a letter:

Your comments in the <u>Business Week</u> article on the difficulty some companies are having recruiting young people with technical skills (October 14, 1981) were provocative and especially interesting to me since I may have been one of the very people you were referring to.

Each of these three openings is superior to the following, which, unfortunately, is the opening most job seekers use in letters:

Are you looking for an experienced marketing executive with ten years of experience and a record of solid accomplishment?

Now, there's nothing *wrong* with this opening. But it's not nearly as intriguing as the other three, and gives the reader a convenient reason for not going any further.

The Presentation. Your second paragraph should get to the meat of your message. It should offer a brief general explanation of why it's worth the reader's time to get together with you, followed by (if you can supply the data) three or four brief examples of accomplishments. Here are some examples:

My background—ten years with an electronics firm—has given me a broad range of experience in all phases of marketing electronics products. Some of my career accomplishments to date include:

* Launching new line of mini-calculators that now are second-largest selling line in field.

* Creating, developing, and supervising the merchandising campaign for the new "little bug" cassette microphone.

* Instrumental, during the four years I worked for Aba Electronics, in boosting gross sales by 30 percent.

I am currently working for a company roughly similar to yours—a $40 million retail chain store. When I began with them five years ago, they had no useable budget, antiquated data processing, and spiraling costs as a result of poor controls. I reversed this pattern and accomplished it within a period of fourteen months.

I have to confess that I do not have any "direct" background in your industry, but I've worked on a number of plastic company accounts, I know the industry, and I feel I could do for your company what I've done for my present company, which includes: (list several accomplishments).

Notice the directness of each of these paragraphs. They *motivate*. They give information that shows off your strong selling points.

Closing. The last part of the letter should express your desire for a direct meeting. Don't make the mistake here of being overapologetic. Don't undersell yourself. For instance, I don't approve of either of the following passages, frequently found in letters sent by candidates:

If you think my qualifications are suitable for the job you're seeking to fill . . .

If you feel that a personal interview would help my chances for being hired . . .

The problem with each of these approaches is that they don't express enough confidence. Be positive in your closing. Show enthusiasm. Some examples follow:

I'd like to be able to discuss some of the problems our industry is having and would be happy at that time to share with you some more of my ideas on how you can increase sales and reduce costs. You can expect my call within a week.

I can appreciate how busy you are, but I wouldn't prevail upon your time if I didn't think it was in our mutual interest to get together and discuss the possibility of my coming to work for your company.

I have a lot of ideas on how an experienced and fresh-thinking training supervisor could help your company during this inflationary period, and I would like the chance to talk them over with you in person. Perhaps we can set up an appointment to meet some time next week? I'll work my schedule around yours.

The Total Effect

Here, finally, are three examples of complete letters:

December 28, 1981

Harlan K. Fieldcroft, President
Widget Industries, Inc.
1800 Washington Street
Fairfield, CT. 06953

Dear Mr. Fieldcroft:

Your comments in the <u>Business Week</u> article on the difficulty some companies are having recruiting young people with technical skills (October 14, 1981) were provocative and especially interesting to me since I may have been one of the very people you were referring to.

As it happens, I'm finishing up my MA degree in electrical engineering, and yours is a firm that has always interested me because of the innovative approach you've taken to the marketing of new products. I think my training could help your company to develop products that would enable you to maintain your leadership in the industry. I would very much welcome the opportunity to discuss the possibility of coming to work for your company, and will contact you within a week or so to see about making the necessary arrangements.

Thank you for your attention and consideration.

Sincerely yours,

Frank Adams

January 5, 1982

Ms. Leslie Robertson
Director of Marketing,
Sun Ray Cosmetics Corp.
48 East 50th Street
New York, N.Y. 10022

Dear Ms. Robertson:

I found the talk you gave earlier this week at the Marketing Women of America luncheon meeting very interesting—particularly your comments about the hesitance of some women to pursue high-level marketing positions. I agree with you that many women fail to pursue opportunities not because the opportunities aren't there, but because of their own uncertainty about their ability to do the job.

Well, I'm very serious about moving into a high-level marketing position. Although I have several years of direct marketing experience, I've been involved in business in one way or another for the past six years. I can handle a lower- to mid-level marketing job right now and am able to make an immediate contribution.

I appreciate how busy you are, but I would very much welcome being able to talk to you personally about a job with Sun Ray. Or, if no position is currently available, I would greatly appreciate the chance to talk with you, in general, about marketing and the cosmetics field.

I'll call your secretary early next week to set up a possible appointment. I appreciate whatever help you're able to give me, and I look forward to meeting with you.

Sincerely yours,

Emily Foster

January 29, 1982

Mr. Edward L. Oxford, President
Oxford Industries, Inc.
160 West Fielding Street
Denver, CO. 86709

Dear Mr. Oxford:

For the past two years, I have been following with a great deal of interest the growth of Oxford Industries, Inc., and I'm writing you today because I think I could play a role in its continued growth over the next several years.

For the past five years, I have been a training supervisor in a $30 million food products company in suburban Chicago. During this period, I have:

* Established training programs that have cut down the employee dismissal rate by 35 percent.
* Introduced a supervisory sensitivity program that has been written up in two trade journals (I enclose the articles).
* Reorganized basic evaluation procedures for supervisors that has cut down on the paperwork they must do by 30 to 40 percent.

I'm thirty-five, am married and have two children. I have 12 years of experience in human relations. I would have no problem relocating and would be happy to come to Denver, at my own expense, to discuss job possibilities with you.

If you feel that a personal meeting might prove mutually beneficial, please contact me at your convenience so that we can set up a specific time and place.

I look forward to hearing from you.

Sincerely yours,

Robert Darwin

Getting Out-of-Town Leads

Looking for a job out of town presents some rather obvious logistical problems, not the least of which is the added expense of travel and phone calls. Yet you may be in an area of the country or in a field in which looking out of town gives you the best chance of finding a good job. Here are some suggestions:

1. *Subscribe to the papers in the two or three cities you're most interested in.*

2. *Get a mail drop in the particular cities.* It's easy and not too expensive. Most telephone answering services will provide you with a local mailing address and even send mail to you. An in-town address won't scare away a potential employer as much as an out-of-town address will.

3. *Get copies of the cities' Yellow Pages.* Have a friend ship them to you, or talk to your local phone company. They might be able to get them for you.

4. *Contact the significant agencies and recruiters in each area.* Send each of them a letter outlining what you're looking for and your background. Include your résumé.

Plan your visits to each city carefully. Telephone recruiters and agencies ahead of time. Do the same with key companies. Interestingly enough, a lot of companies will be impressed by the fact that you're from out of town but are looking in their city—especially when you're making the trip at *your* expense. Early in the interview make known your willingness to pay your own relocation expenses, if necessary.

Other Lead Sources

There are a number of other sources for leads in addition to the ones I've already listed. I'll mention them briefly, but keep in mind that these are sources you shouldn't spend much time pursuing unless you have the time or everything else you're doing is producing no results.

1. *Your college placement office.* Worth a visit, if for no other reason than to get names of people you might contact for job leads.

2. *State employment agencies.* Usually a depressing experience because the leads are for low-level jobs.

3. *Situation-wanted ads*. There's mixed opinion on these kinds of ads. My feeling is that if nothing else is working, try one; but place it in a trade magazine, not a general newspaper. Spend time on the language. Make it strong but not gimmicky. (Then again, if the strong approach doesn't work, go ahead and make it gimmicky: what do you have to lose?)

4. *Company outplacement*. More and more firms are now offering outplacement services for dismissed employees. The intentions are good but, from what I've seen, often the execution leaves quite a bit to be desired. Given a choice, I'd suggest that you take extra severance pay in lieu of the outplacement service.

VI

Coming Out on Top in the Job Interview: The Getting Ready Part

*The first person interviewed is often
the last person considered.*

The job interview is the moment of truth in job hunting—so crucial and organic an aspect of getting hired that entire books have been devoted to the subject. Yet interviews are probably the trickiest aspect of job hunting in which to dispense advice.

The problem is that the interview is very much a game—a game, moreover, in which the rules are constantly changing. Ostensibly, you and the interviewer (sometimes other people are involved, too) are having a civilized conversation. You greet one another. There's some small talk. The interviewer asks you some questions. You answer them. The interviewer asks you if *you* have any questions. The questions get answered. And so forth.

But while all of this is going on, the interviewer is playing out his or her role in the game: paying attention not only to what you're saying but to how you're responding. The interviewer is making an evaluation, computing nearly everything you say and do, the better to judge whether your ability, experience, education, and personality fit the job and the company. The interviewer *knows* you're doing your best to create a positive impression. The interviewer *knows* that as hard as the two of you may try to make the interview seem natural and unforced, the interview is, by nature, an unnatural and forced situation. Much of how the interviewer evaluates you will be determined not so much by the qualifications you enumerate and the personal qualities you exhibit during the

interview, but by your *interview performance in general*.
How you play the game!

So what we're going to be talking about throughout this
chapter is the job interview as a performance in itself. You
already know—or should know—the qualities that make you
special. You already know—or should know—the skills and
the attributes it takes to do the job being offered. Your task in
the interview is to make a sale: to sell the person (or persons)
who interviews you on the idea you already know ahead of
time: that you're the best person for the job.

Taking Control

There are two ways to approach a job interview. One is to
be passive: to sit there and answer whatever questions you're
given to the best of your ability. The other is to be active: to
take control of the interview, to give the interviewer what *you*
want to give, not necessarily what the interviewer is trying to
find out. One of the most successful insurance salesmen I
know had an interesting theory that applies as much to getting
hired as it does to selling insurance. "Other insurance salesmen," he said, "present facts and answer questions. I inspire
confidence."

The way you inspire confidence in an interview is to give
the interviewer every reason to believe that you can handle
the job for which you're being considered, and little reason to
believe that you *can't*. You supply these reasons (one way or
the other) with much more than the answers you give to
questions. You supply reasons with the way you look, with
the enthusiasm you show or don't show, with the personability
you show or don't show, with the energy, the confidence,
and the ambition you show or don't show.

You are in control. The interviewer is asking the questions,
but if you know what to expect and how to sell yourself, you
can take control of the interview in a way that will give the
interviewer reasons to hire you.

So let's put ourselves for the moment in the chair of the
person—or persons—sitting across the desk or table from you
at a typical interview.

I can tell you from more than thirty years of experience that virtually everything an interviewer is concerned about in a typical interview situation boils down, in the end, to one of three questions:

1. *Can you do the job?*

2. *Will you do the job?*

3. *Do you fit in with the company style?*

Underlying these three questions is a fourth factor: what the interviewer has to gain or lose by hiring you or by recommending you to be hired. I know some interviewers who need very strong positive answers to all three questions before they'll hire you or recommend you for hiring. Other interviewers will take a chance if you're particularly strong in one or two of the areas covered by the three questions above and not necessarily all of them. You never know until you get to the interview which type of interviewer you're going to encounter.

But now you know what the interviewer is looking for. Regardless of the questions you are asked—and you may be asked any one of three hundred different questions—the answers you give must be plugged into one of these three areas: *your ability to do the job, your willingness to do the job, your suitability for the job and the company*. Every answer you give should, one way or another, say one of the following three things:

1. *I am able to do this job.*

2. *I am willing to do this job.*

3. *I can fit in.*

The more your answers and actions in a job interview express these three statements, the more control you are exercising in the interview and the better your chances of winning the ultimate prize of an interview—a job offer.

Sizing Up the Situation

The main reason why most job candidates fall short in the job interview is that they don't inspire confidence. They give the interviewer more reasons to say no than to say yes.

In most cases, the reason is a simple matter of fear—the fear of failing. I've seen it happen hundreds of times in my career. Candidates with marvelous qualifications lose out not because they couldn't do the job or even lacked the confidence that they could do the job. They lose out because their confidence didn't come through in the interview situation. They didn't "sell" themselves convincingly enough. They didn't inspire confidence.

Let's tackle the root of the problem: the nervousness most people feel any time there is pressure on them to perform. There is a job opening and you want the job, maybe need it very badly. The interview is an obstacle. Can you be blamed for being anxious?

Not at all. In fact, a little anxiety is good for you. Ask any championship athlete, and they'll tell you that what *really* worries them before an important match or tournament is not feeling any nerves.

The challenge, of course, is to *control* this anxiety: to make it work for you, not defeat you. One thing that might help is to keep in mind that you have nothing to lose in a job interview. *Nothing*. Even if you don't get the job, you won't be much worse off than you were a short while before you heard about it.

If you get turned down—and, remember, most people who get interviewed get turned down—there will be other interviews, other chances to do what you may not have done as well as you wanted to do in this last interview.

As hard as it may seem to do, it's possible to divorce the significance of the interview—what is at stake—from the interview itself. Athletes do it all the time. "I'm not competing for the Wimbledon championship," tennis great Fred Perry used to say. "I'm just going out to play a game of tennis."

Do the same thing in a job interview. Forget about whether or not you're going to get the job. Concentrate on the interview itself. *Get good at the skill.* Learn from past mistakes. See every interview you go on as a chance to put into practice what you learned at your last interview. If you handle the interview well, the job offer will take care of itself. Don't even think about the outcome: it will only interfere.

Develop confidence in yourself as a job interviewee. I'm serious! I've known dozens and dozens of people whose employment record had little to recommend them. Yet, get these people in a one-to-one interview situation, and they were world-beaters. They were offered jobs. They didn't always keep these jobs, unfortunately, but that's another story. "I *know* I don't have the qualifications," I remember one young woman telling me years ago, "but it's never been a problem in the past. Set up the interview."

Confident job candidates know that in spite of what a lot of the books and articles about job interviewing might lead you to believe, the person doing the interviewing, much of the time, is *not* a professional interviewer schooled in "secret" techniques. He or she is simply a person with a problem: hiring somebody to fill a job. Confident job candidates know that far from fighting your attempts to take control over the interview situation, most interviewers will *welcome* it: you're making their job easier. Confident job candidates know that they, the candidates, know more about interviewing, about the job, and about themselves than the interviewer knows. They know that as long as the subject of discussion is one of the areas the candidate knows more about than the interviewer, the candidate (not the interviewer) holds the upper hand.

Make it *your* business to develop the same confidence: it's not nearly as hard as you might think.

Being Prepared

Confidence is rooted in knowledge, knowledge, in turn, is rooted in preparation. If you've been following the guidelines I've set down throughout this book, you know the qualities and attributes that set you apart from other candidates. You know the qualities and attributes needed in the kind of job you're looking for. The job interview introduces a new element: the company offering the job.

Never go into any interview unless you've thoroughly researched the company offering the job. You should know its products, its size, its top executives, its growth pattern, its recent financial performance, its strengths, and its weaknesses.

For large companies, this kind of information is easy to come by: a morning in the library, going through various business directories like Dun & Bradstreet's, Standard & Poor's and Moody's Manuals, should give you basic information. Check through the *Reader's Guide to Periodical Literature* for a list of recent articles that may have appeared on the company in publications like *Time, Newsweek, Business Week, Dun's Review,* or *Financial World.* Get hold of the trade publications that deal with the industry in which the company is involved; you might discover some interesting data. At the very least, get your hands on the company's annual report and on any brochures or internal publications (newsletters, company papers, etc.) you can latch onto. The simplest way to get an annual report is to call a stockbroker you know, the secretary of the company, or the company's public relations department.

Another source of information is the company's 10-K form. A 10-K form is a form that every public company has to file with the Securities and Exchange Commission. In some cases, it's little more than a financial statement; in other cases, you'll find such information as the salary the company pays to its top officers—useful information to have. You could probably get one of these forms from the Securities and Exchange Commission, but it may take time. If you're in a hurry, there's a company in New York that will send you the 10-K on any company in one day for a modest fee. The company is called National Investment, Inc., and its address is 80 Wall St., New York, N.Y. 10005.

Read the material you gather with an inquiring eye. Look for trends. See if you can discern a company philosophy. Is the company adopting a new marketing philosophy, changing its product lines, experiencing certain kinds of problems you might be able to help solve? Find out about the president and other officers. Jot down whatever information you get on note cards, or, better still, in a notebook bought for this purpose only.

See if you can locate somebody who knows the company well. It might be an employee or an ex-employee, or a professional person who does work for them. See what you can dig out of these people. Many firms, although they won't admit it, have a preconceived idea of who "their" kind of people are. The "style" usually filters down from the chief executive. You may not fit the mold, but it doesn't hurt to find out what the mold is.

Discovering somebody who knows the company pretty well is especially important if it's a smaller company that hasn't generated much publicity. You may find when you go to the library and consult the various indexes that there is virtually no material about this particular company. This being the case, you are pretty much forced to go directly to the source. Talk to the person who has either set up the interview for you or is, in fact, going to conduct the interview. Explain the problem. Tell him—or her—you'd like some information that isn't confidential about the company before the interview and would they be kind enough to send you whatever they can. Most executives will oblige you.

Don't overlook, or take for granted, this research aspect of the interview. *Our surveys show that not being familiar with the company with whom you're interviewing will hurt your chances with as many as 75 percent of the interviews you may encounter.*

Getting Yourself Ready for the Game

At the beginning of this chapter, I said that the key to doing well in a job interview is the ability to give a performance. At the same time, however, you have to be yourself. What I'm talking about here is not as paradoxical as it may seem.

Think about the last time you took part in a sport, whether it was golf or tennis or bowling. Or played bridge. You were performing there, too, and yet you were being yourself. You were playing a role, whether of golfer, tennis player, bowler, or bridge player.

A job interview is a game because it represents a reality within a reality. It has rules. It asks the people involved with it to play certain roles. The person who interviews you is a person, not an interviewer: he or she is playing the role of interviewer. And you are not a job candidate: you are a person who, in this particular situation, is *playing the role of job candidate*.

Appreciate the job interview situation in these role-playing terms, and it will help you immeasurably when it comes to presenting the best side of yourself in an interview. Understand the game. Understand the role you must play in it. You're not faking or being insincere when you play this role the way it should be played. The game, after all, is *real*—and so must the role you play in it be.

The best way to play this role is to *be* the person the role calls for. Who gets the job? Our surveys show that the single most influential factor in the job interview situation is not your experience or your qualification, but your personality—*how you present yourself during the interview*. How you look, how you communicate your ideas, how well you listen, how much enthusiasm you generate.

You have a personality, for better or worse, and it's not a *fixed* personality. I know boisterous people who are often subdued, and I know painfully shy people who, under the right set of circumstances, can become outlandishly outgoing. You have a great deal of range within your own personality. Chances are you don't have to *change* anything about yourself when you go into a job interview: you simply have to present the best and most saleable side of that personality.

How Role Playing Can Work for You

If you don't already have one, buy or get hold of a cassette tape recorder. You can probably get one for $25 or even less. Don't worry too much about the sound quality: you're not going to be recording any piano concertos on it. (If you own or have access to a video camera and playback machine, that's even better.)

Once you get it, conduct this little experiment. Find a quiet spot in your house and pretend for a moment that you're on a job interview and you are asked, as often happens at such interviews, to "tell us something about yourself." Turn the tape recorder on and talk into it for three or four minutes, free associating as you go.

Now play it back and listen. Really listen. What if you didn't know the person whose voice you're listening to? What conclusions would you draw about this person, based on the comments alone? Would you consider the person sure of himself or herself, perceptive, articulate? If your answer is definitely yes, you probably have no problem presenting yourself. My guess, though, is that you'll be a little disappointed by what you hear.

Don't be. Unless you have special training or are in a field that requires you to be "on" a lot of the time, there's no reason why you should be especially impressive or effective at "selling yourself." Don't be dismayed. You have time to get better at it.

Now I'd like you to try the same exercise again, but this time, I want you to play a role. I want you to play the role of a confident person. It doesn't matter whether you are or aren't a confident person. You know what confidence is and what a confident person sounds like: behave like one into the tape recorder. *Overdo* it.

When you play the tape back a second time, you're going to be surprised. You will *sound* confident. What's more, you should be able to recognize a difference between the confidence level of certain things you say and the confidence level of other things.

Do one more thing. Think for a moment about all the points that, in your judgment, make you the best candidate to be hired. Write them down. In fact, go back to the notes you used in drafting your résumé. Once you have a half-dozen or so of these qualities, talk them into the tape recorder, mentioning the quality first—i.e., "I'm a very hard worker"— and then saying a few words to back the statement up.

Now play it back and evaluate it. How believable did you sound? If you were an interviewer and this tape were all you had to judge by, how would you evaluate the person you're listening to? Just as important, what might you do to make that person *more* believable?

Working with a tape recorder in this way does wonders. I know because I've used one myself in preparing for television and radio appearances. I don't memorize anything. I simply interview myself. I ask questions; I give answers. Then I listen and evaluate myself.

Rehearse your part in the job interview. When you're alone in your car, answer questions aloud—with or without a tape recorder. Take your time, be as articulate as you can.

The beauty of this approach is that *you* are making the changes consistent with your personality and consistent with what you're comfortable with. But don't force it. Be yourself—just a more convincing, confident, and articulate version of yourself.

Fielding the Key Questions

Most of the conversation that takes place in a job interview will revolve around questions you get asked by the interviewer. The nature—and the intensity—of these questions will vary according to the type of interview. The questions that get asked during interviews with personnel executives will be more general than the questions that get asked when you're across from somebody who is making the hiring decision. Your answers to decision making executives, moreover, won't have to be as detailed, and there won't be as much give and take in the general pattern of questions and answers. In personnel interviews, where the purpose is either to screen you out or send you ahead for future interviews, questions will be asked in a more or less one-at-a-time fashion. Later on, you can expect questions keyed to the kind of answers you give.

Should You Tell the Truth?

I've known job placement specialists who've encouraged their clients to lie when confronted with a potentially damaging question. I've known other specialists who advocate complete candor. I myself have never and would never come out and tell any job candidate to lie deliberately but neither do I recommend that you *volunteer* irrelevant information about yourself that may hurt your chances, or to dwell on your negative features simply because they happen to be true. Never forget, your "negatives" hurt you more than your "positives" help.

There is the principle to keep in mind when you're answering tough questions: steering the information away from a possibly negative picture of yourself to a positive aspect of yourself.

Here's another example. The interviewer asks if you've ever worked directly in a particular field: "Have you ever worked with people in the food industry?" The truth here is that you haven't. I say, answer the question truthfully, but don't just leave the answer lying there. Build on it. "No, I haven't," you might say. "But I've worked with a lot of people in the liquor industry, and I know a good deal about the food industry . . ." Do you see the principle? Here, you've given a truthful answer but defused truth if the truth doesn't work to your advantage.

The Most Frequently Asked Questions and How to Answer Them

I have in my files nearly three hundred questions, any one of which you might get asked in a job interview. Fortunately, many of the questions are variations of other questions; and, besides, I would no more expect you to prepare answers to three hundred questions than I would ask you to run up the stairs in the Empire State Building.

So, what I've done is to pick twenty-five of the questions that get asked the most frequently in job interviews. In each case, I've tried to suggest what the interviewer might be looking for in the question, and then to suggest a strategy for answering it.

1. Tell me about yourself . . .

This is a typical ice-breaker in many interview situations. Interviewers like it because it gives them a good initial "feeling" about you. They figure if you can't be articulate when you're talking about yourself, you're not going to be very articulate about anything.

Generally, it isn't so much what you say when you answer this question that's important, it's *how* you say it. Don't fumble with it. A good way to start an answer might be to come right out and say that you're darn good at what you do. "Well," you could say, "people tell me I'm a very good administrator." Having made this statement, however, you now have an obligation to back it up. How well you back up your general statements is another thing many interviewers are going to be looking for. "I'm organized," you might say. "I know how to delegate. I work well under pressure."

As long as you stay within reasonable bounds, don't worry about tooting your own horn. The interviewer knows you're not going to emphasize your negative points. But concentrate on those things about yourself that *relate to the job you're being interviewed for,* remembering (again) to back up your general statements with specific details. Instead of merely saying, "I get along well with others," and letting it go at that, give a couple of specific examples that illustrate how well you get along with others. "I've always had a good rapport with the people I work for and the people I supervise. In fact, I'm very close friends with one of my former bosses."

So, the main things to bear in mind when you're answering this question are:

- Stress only positive features.
- Back up general statements with proof—specific examples that illustrate the statements. Stress accomplishments.

- Try to key most of what you say to the qualifications needed for the job that's open.
- Keep it brief—no more than two or three minutes.
- When you've finished, ask the interviewer if he or she needs to know any more.

2. What do you think of our little operation here?

Here's a question you're likely to get asked when you're on your third or fourth interview for the same job. It sounds innocent, but answer with a good deal of care.

The conservative way to handle the question is to finesse it. Tell the interviewer you haven't had much of a chance to draw any real conclusions, but from what you've seen, you're impressed—it looks like the kind of place where you could be very happy.

If you've noticed some things that do indeed need to be changed and you figure you're the person to do the changing, it isn't a bad idea to say that as much as you like what you've seen, you think you could make some positive changes. But be careful how you say this. No matter how strong a candidate you are, or how badly the company wants you, it's suicide to come into an interview acting as if you're Wyatt Earp come to clean up Dodge City. One way you might handle the problem is to say something like: "Well, from what I've seen, I'm very impressed. But what's important to me is that you seem to have some of the same interesting problems we were having at my former company."

Expressing yourself this way accomplishes several things: first, it takes the edge out of your criticism by making it seem as if a lot of companies have the same problem; second, it indicates, indirectly, your familiarity with the problem and implies your ability to solve it; third, it gives the interviewer the option of pursuing the matter or dropping it. The ball is in their court.

Whatever you do, watch what you say about any of the people connected with the company you've met so far. As far as you're concerned, they're all terrific people and you see no problem at all in getting along with them. Occasionally, you might run into an interviewer who wants to see how much of a hatchet person you are. The conversation sometimes goes like this:

INTERVIEWER: Don't you think some of these people need somebody to build a fire under them?

YOU: As I said, it's hard to tell about people unless you've had a chance to work with them for a while.

INTERVIEWER: Would you have any compunctions about firing people?

YOU: Well, sometimes you don't have a choice. But I look on firing as a last resort.

3. What is it about this job that interests you most?

It may well be that you're getting desperate for *any* job, but nobody expects you to give this answer. Play the game. What the interviewer is generally looking for here is how much homework you've done with respect to the company. Unload with both barrels. Discuss what you like about the company's marketing philosophy (or whatever) and explain why you like it. Talk about the company's products and why you think there's such a future in them. Keep personal considerations (it's close to home, etc.) out of this answer. Leave the interviewer with the impression that you and the job are an ideal match!

4. This is a very high-pressured job. Do you think you're up to it?

Another one of those questions in which *how* you answer is as important as what you say. Don't be in too much of a hurry to give a blanket "Yes." Ask the interviewer to describe the kind of pressure he or she means. Maybe the pressure *is* too much for you. Maybe you don't want it. Either way, underplay it. Instead of talking about how superbly you perform under pressure, indicate that pressure has never been a problem for you, that in a lot of ways you *enjoy* pressure. If you can cite an example or two to back up your point, all the better. I remember a candidate who smiled when I asked him this question and said: "I'd be bored without pressure."

5. What do you see yourself doing five years from now?

Read this question to mean: Are you going to stick with us for a while and then jump somewhere else? Hedge here, and no one will fault you for it. "Well, I like what I do. I see myself doing more of it and doing it better."

6. What do you consider your major strengths?

You *know* what your major strengths are and how they relate to the job, so you should never have any trouble answering this question. Just remember to back up general statements now and then with some specific examples. "I think I handle people well. When I worked at ABC, people were always commenting on the high morale in my department. The one thing I do well with people is to listen to them . . ." To repeat, stick with the strengths that relate to the job.

7. What do you consider your major weaknesses?

You're not in group therapy or at an est meeting, so play this question by the book. Of course you have weaknesses. Everybody has weaknesses. But you don't feel as if your weaknesses have ever interfered much with your ability to do a good job. Some of the "safe" weaknesses to reveal, if true, are: you're impatient with people who don't work hard; you sometimes get too involved with your work; you sometimes don't know when to throw in the towel.

8. Why do you want to leave your present job?

Assuming, that is, you have a present job. Play this one safe, too. For example, you "like" your present job, and you think a lot of your present company and the people you're working with. On the other hand, you see *this* job (the job you're being interviewed for) as offering you a better opportunity to grow.

9. *Why did you have to leave your last job?*

The fact may be that you were fired, and chances are the interviewer *knows* you were fired and is simply interested in how you'll handle the question. *Never make excuses.* Never paint yourself as a victim or a scapegoat. ''There were a lot of organizational changes,'' you might say, ''and things just didn't work out after a while. I have no hard feelings. I learned a lot, and I might have been ready for a change.''

10. *Do you think you can get along with . . . ?*

This is a question you're likely to get asked when you're being interviewed for a job at a small company dominated by one person. The interviewer, of course, knows that the top person is *difficult* to get along with but wants to see your reaction anyway. A good, safe answer is: ''Let me put it this way. I've never worked for anybody I couldn't get along with.''

11. *What sort of money are you looking for?*

The stock response here is to try to beg the question. ''Salary is something we can talk about once I get a better feel of what's involved.'' If the interviewer persists, give your present salary. Don't lie. Always talk salary in general terms, ''in the neighborhood of the high 30s.''

12. *I'm a little worried about your lack of . . .*

It might be experience or training. Don't be intimidated by this question, because it's a good sign. It means the interviewer likes you generally but has a reservation or two. Grant that you understand the concern he or she might have, and then immediately give the interviewer *something* concrete that can put his or her mind at ease. ("I can see where you might be concerned about that, but all I've been doing, really, for the past two years is handle heavy-equipment accounts . . .") By the way, this is a question you *must* be prepared to answer well.

13. We work a lot of late nights here. Is that going to cause any trouble at home?

If it *isn't* a problem let the interviewer know. "Of course it isn't. I'm very lucky to have a family that is very independent. The idea of working late has never been a problem for me." As much as possible, keep personal family problems out of any interview discussion. Then again, do you *want* to work late all the time?

14. You've been out of work for a long time, haven't you?

You have indeed, and there's no point in denying it. Turn the question into a plus. "It's true," you might say, "but I think I've used the time very well. I've become much better at . . . (list what you've accomplished during this period)." Let the interviewer know that you've been particular, that you've turned down offers—if it's true.

15. What do you like to do in your spare time?

An innocent question most of the time, but sometimes a fishing expedition to find out whether your leisure pursuits could interfere with your commitment to work. Don't be in a hurry to show how rounded an individual you are, or how good a tennis player you happen to be. Don't mention that you like to scuba dive or go sky diving unless your interviewer has a photograph on his desk of himself (or herself) sky diving or scuba diving. On the other hand, don't say you don't have *any* hobbies: you'll give the impression of being too narrow. One good way to start the answer to this question is with: "Well, when I get the time, I like to do a little . . ."

16. I see you've just gotten divorced. It's not going to inter-fere with your work, is it?

The interviewer probably has no business asking this, but if you do get asked it, don't make an issue. "Divorces are never easy," you might say, "but things are under control. I certainly don't see any problem where working is concerned." Incidentally, our Burke survey shows that divorce is likely to be a negative factor in your hiring chances in only about 15 percent of the interviews you go on. Still, go into the inter-view expecting the interviewer to have a negative attitude and be ready to defuse it. Stress the stability of your social life. Mention how civilized a relationship you have with your ex-spouse.

17. Have you hired or fired many people?

Could be a trick question: an executive, after all, who has to do a lot of hiring and firing might be difficult to work with. On the other hand, the interviewer may be concerned that your background hasn't adequately prepared you for the hir-ing or firing responsibility in this particular job. However you answer this question, give the impression that you recognize that firing people is a necessary—if unpleasant—part of execu-tive responsibility and that you have good judgment when it comes to people.

18. You've had quite a few jobs in your career. Why?

The interviewer is worried about your stability and your loyalty. Your answer should address itself to both these con-cerns. If the facts can back you up, point out that most of your job changing took place several years ago but that your record over the past, say, three years has been a lot more stable. Another approach is to point out the one or two jobs in which you've stayed for a reasonably long period of time, and try to indicate similarities between those situations and the job for which you're now being considered. Whatever you do, don't answer this question in a way that will suggest you're blaming others for your inability to stay at one place for very long. Be prepared to spell out the reasons for each termination.

19. You have too much experience for this job. Why would you want it?

Sometimes this question indicates an interviewer's sincere concern that you're not reaching high enough in your aspirations. Other times, the interviewer is worried that something about your personality is holding you back. Don't be defensive. Make the abundance of experience you have a "plus." "It's nice of you to say that," you might reply, "but I don't see it as a problem. I really like this field, and I'd much rather go into a new job with a lot of experience than with little experience. It gives me a chance to be creative in the job."

What you *don't* do in answering this question is to downplay your experience. Experience is a feather in your cap: don't let the interviewer turn it into a liability. Indeed, never answer any question in a way that disparages any of your qualifications.

20. You've been with the same firm for so many years, how can you now cope with a new firm?

The interviewer is concerned that you may not be ambitious enough, that you got stale at your last job and that's why they let you go. Remember, though, loyalty is an *asset*, not a liability, so don't waste this opportunity to showcase the asset. The safe answer here is to point out that while it's true you've been with the same firm for a long time, you've always felt as if you were "growing" and you never felt as if you were "stuck." Point out, if true, that even though you were with the same firm for so many years, you worked in a number of different environments and that you see no problem at all adjusting to a new firm. Here's a good chance, too, to show how much you know about the firm for whose job you're being considered. "I know a lot about your company," you might say. "And I've thought a lot about how I might work out here, and I think I could fit in very well."

21. I'm surprised your salary isn't higher, considering every- thing you say you've done.

This is a polite way of suggesting that you might be exagger- ating your accomplishments, in light of your salary. One way to answer the question is to tell the interviewer that while the company you're now working for is fine in a lot of way, it isn't known for paying high salaries (which, of course, is one of the reasons you're looking elsewhere).

A generally good line to take here is to agree with the interviewer but finesse the explanation: "This is one of the problems when you work, don't you think? You have to bal- ance how much you like what you do with how much money they pay you. One of the reasons I'm interested in *your* firm is that it seems to key salary to accomplishment."

22. Tell me what you think _____ really involves?

The blank is your specialty, whether it's accounting, advertis- ing, marketing, public relations, selling, or anything else. This is the classic "big picture" question. The interviewer is trying to get a fix on whether you've given thought to the essence of your profession or specialty. It's an important question, and you should have an answer ready for it.

23. Do you have any problems following company policy?

The interviewer wants to find out if you're a potential trou- blemaker. You're not, of course. Cite the fact, if true, that you've never had any problems following company policy in any company you've ever worked for.

24. What was it about your last job that bothered you the most?

Talk in generalities. Lack of challenge and growth are two good standard responses. You probably have others just as appropriate.

25. What was it you liked best about your last job?

A good answer might be "the people." You got along well with them. You liked the fact that they trusted your judgment. This is an excellent question in which to emphasize the points that will make you good for *this* job.

Here are twenty-five additional questions you should be prepared to answer:

1. What motivates you?
2. What are your long-term goals?
3. Do you think you'd like my job?
4. How creative a problem solver are you?
5. Can you motivate people?
6. How would you rate yourself as a leader?
7. What was your favorite subject in school?
8. How well did you do in school?
9. What kind of jobs did you like best as a kid?
10. What would you say are your most important accomplishments to date?
11. What kind of people do you like to associate with?
12. Do you have much of a temper?
13. What kind of a contribution do you think you could make to this firm?
14. Why do you want to change careers at your age?
15. How much of a self-starter are you?
16. If you could be in your own business, would you prefer it to corporate life?
17. How long do you think you'd be happy in this job before you started thinking about promotion?
18. What's your health like?
19. Do you really *enjoy* work?

20. Would you work if you were independently wealthy?
21. How involved are you with your children?
22. How do you think your wife (husband) is going to feel about your taking this job?
23. How sensitive are you to criticism?
24. What's the most difficult challenge you've faced in your life?
25. What are you doing now to improve yourself?

The Art of Persuasion

We all know how to talk, but most of us have never fully mastered the art of communication. You talk with your mouth. You communicate with your mouth, your ears, your eyes, your hands, your posture. Talking is saying something to somebody else. Communicating is interacting with that person, or those people you're talking with. It's being sensitive to the feedback from these people that tells you whether what you're saying is making any impact or not.

The object of a job interview is not to "tell" the interviewer about yourself. It's to communicate to the interviewer the three things I mentioned earlier: your ability, your willingness, and your suitability.

You don't become an effective communicator overnight. You work at it. And I wouldn't presume to suggest that on the basis of the advice I'm giving you in this book, you can master this difficult art. But let me mention and elaborate on a few aspects of communication that relate directly to the job interview, and suggest some ways you can improve—if not completely master—your skills in each of these areas.

Personalizing Your Presentation

Interviewers bring to the interview situation not only their own techniques of getting information, but their own personality quirks and their own prejudices. Much of your ability to communicate persuasively will depend on how effectively you can tailor your presentation to the personality of the interviewer.

What I'm talking about here doesn't mean having any number of pre-programmed "approaches" ready. It's better to trot out the presentation that suits a particular personality type. No. It means being able to "read" your interviewer early on, and to shape your conversation and your answers in ways that are keyed to how the interviewer responds.

For example, many interviewers are very direct and pragmatic in their basic approach to their work. They tend to ask specific questions and to expect specific answers. Other interviewers are more analytical: they want more than short, precise answers—they want you to elaborate a little more on the answers. Certain interviewers are highly company-oriented. Their main concern is whether or not you're going to fit into the "family." Personnel executives tend to fall into this category.

Not all interviewers, of course, can be easily classified, but it's been my experience that most fall into one of four general categories. I'll describe each of the "types," tell you how you can recognize them, then give you an idea of the best way to approach each.

1. *The Target-Directed Interviewer*. Interviewers who fall into this category tend to be direct, businesslike, and a little impersonal in their basic interviewing approach. They're not terribly interested in you as a person—only in what you can bring to a job. They ask their questions succinctly. They're impatient with lengthy and discursive answers. They'll frequently interrupt you if they feel you're drifting away from the point.

Target-Directed interviewers are easy to spot. They tend to be abrupt and somewhat hurried when they greet you. They'll *tell* you, not invite you, where to sit. They won't spend much time with preliminary small talk. Usually, but not always, you won't see a lot of personal photographs either on the walls or on the desk. They're all business.

It's easy to be intimidated by this type of an interviewer. They are not interested in putting you at ease, and are not usually responsive. They'll ask a question, listen to an answer, maybe nod, then go on to the next question.

The key to handling yourself when you're being interviewed by such a person is to present your answers as briefly as you can, but not allow yourself to be bullied into shortchanging them. Stick mainly with facts. Leave personal observations out of the conversation as much as you can. Don't allow yourself to be rushed. The more numbers and hard data you can give to such an interviewer the better. If, toward the end of the session, this interviewer asks you bluntly: "Can you handle this job?", don't hesitate. "I know I can handle it," you should say. What impresses the Target-Directed Interviewer is directness, a clear sense of purpose, and confidence. What bothers the Target-Directed Interviewer is vagueness, blue-skying, and indecision.

2. *The All-in-the-Family Interviewer.* The All-in-the-Family Interviewer should remind you a little of a nice uncle (aunt) you used to know—the sort of person who liked everybody and wanted everybody to like him or her. Whether you can handle a particular job is important to this interviewer, but not as important perhaps as how comfortably you'll fit into the "family" atmosphere of a certain department or an entire company.

This type of interviewer will usually give you a warm greeting, and go out of his or her way to make sure you're comfortable and at ease. You'll probably see family photographs on the desk, and company plaques on the wall. The All-in-the-Family Interviewer will say things like "our people" and mention the president of the company over again.

Whenever you're being interviewed by somebody who fits this type, make sure you emphasize your "team-player" attributes. Show the interviewer that you're people-oriented. Use "we" instead of "I" when talking about your accomplishments at your last job. Let the interviewer know that one of the reasons you're interested in this company is the working atmosphere is known to be warm and friendly. Get the interviewer to see that you're "their" kind of person.

3. *The Thinking Person's Interviewer.* The Thinking Person's Interviewer takes a deliberate and thorough approach to interviewing and is usually interested as much in *how* you did or intend to do things as in what you did or intend to do.

Unlike the Target-Directed Interviewer, this person wants you to answer certain questions at length and will feel uneasy if your answers are too abrupt and non-specific.

Interviewers who fit this type will not be as insensitive as Target-Directed interviewers, but won't be as warm, either, as All-in-the-Family–type interviewers. You will sense a certain detachment in them. They'll ask more theoretical questions. They may want to know, for example, your philosophy of the field you're in.

Above all, try to be as logical in your answers as you can when you're dealing with a Thinking Person's Interviewer. This interviewer, remember, isn't so much interested in hearing you say that you're able to do something or willing to do something. This interviewer wants to be told *how* you intend to do it.

4. *The Make-It-Easy-for-Me Interviewer*. Make-It-Easy-for-Me interviewers are the most difficult of the four types to deal with because they tend to be the most unpredictable. This person isn't comfortable with decision making (and is probably hard to work for). Make-It-Easy-for-Me interviewers are likely to make snap judgments early on and base perceptions throughout the interview on that initial impression.

A person who falls into this category will probably be a little unfocused when you first are introduced. Look for a somewhat disorganized office—a desk that's filled with piles of papers. You'll find this type of interviewer fairly easy to deal with if you indicate a good measure of responsiveness early on. You may be shown a new photograph the interviewer has just bought for his or her office, or be told a story that has nothing to do with the job. Respond enthusiastically.

Your best tack during the interview itself is to let the Make-It-Easy-for-Me Interviewer do most of the talking. People who fall into this category *love* an audience. Give them the stage.

Learning How to Listen

When I was a young CPA apprentice looking to change jobs, I was interviewed by an old-timer at one of the fine medium-sized accounting firms. After we exchanged some small talk, he asked me one question: "Mr. Half, when is a sale a sale?"

I'd been out of college about a year and I figured I knew accounting theory as well as anybody. So I spoke for about ten minutes on the relationship between accounting and merchandise sold. I was convinced as I spoke that the interviewer was going to be impressed by my comprehensive knowledge, so I told him everything—everything, that is, except what he wanted to hear.

"Mr. Half," he interrupted. "All I wanted you to say was, 'A sale is a sale when the merchandise is shipped.'"

I didn't get the job. Why? Because I didn't really listen to the question. I was so intent upon overwhelming the interviewer with my knowledge, with impressing him, that I heard what I wanted to hear in his question, and not what he asked.

To communicate well you have to listen—*really* listen. The more closely you listen to the interviewer, the more closely the interviewer will listen to you.

Make sure you understand each question that's asked you. If you're not sure what the interviewer asked, request that the question be repeated. Don't make the mistake many job candidates make of interrupting an interviewer in the middle of a question—of presenting an answer before the question is complete. Let the question register. Think a second or two before answering it.

Make sure, too, that you listen closely to what the interviewer is saying in general conversation. It isn't always easy in a pressure situation to pay attention. Your mind drifts; you think about something silly you said a minute or two earlier and in the process lose track of what the interviewer is saying *now*. Train yourself to look the interviewer in the eye as he or she is speaking—not constantly, but enough to register the fact that you're listening.

Be a *responsive* listener. Nod. Agree. Shake your head if you've been given a piece of information that warrants that kind of response. Listening is not a passive act—it's active. Stay involved in the conversation and you'll find, as a bonus, that your tension level will drop.

A Few Hints on Becoming a Better "Listener"

• *Don't rush the person talking to you.* If the interviewer has a slow delivery, don't speed it up, as some people do, by finishing the person's sentence, or by starting your answer before the question is finished.

• *Keep strong emotional responses under control.* The minute you get angry, you stop listening. You may have the *right* to get angry, but keep your focus on what the person is saying, not on how you want to react.

• *Ignore distractions.* The secretary walks in while the interviewer is talking to you. If the interviewer keeps talking, don't you break the contact by looking over at the secretary.

• *Don't overdo your attention energy.* Eye contact is important, but if you overdo it, you'll make the speaker uneasy and you'll lose track of the conversation. You can indicate responsiveness by glancing down now and then and nodding, to suggest that you're absorbing what's being said to you.

Body Language: Picking Up the Cues

Body language—the psychological signals people give off with their bodies—has been an interest of mine for years, and while I'm not sold on how pure a science it is, it's certainly a useful tool to have with you when you go into a job interview.

The basic idea is to keep an eye on the interviewer's body motions while the two of you are talking. Certain body movements could indicate that you're boring the interviewer or getting into an area that's making the person uneasy. As I said, it's an art, not a science, but here are some of the warning signs and the body signals that indicate them:

1. *The interviewer is bored.* Look for fidgeting motions, playing with some object on the desk. Tapping the fingers is another sign. When you see this, try to change the subject. *Ask* questions to get the interviewer back into the flow of the interview.

2. *The interviewer is distracted.* According to body lan-

guage specialists, distraction shows up when the person you're talking to has trouble making eye contact with you. The person stares off to the right or left of you, or else down at an object on the desk.

3. *The interviewer is getting upset.* "Defensive," signals include the following: crossing the arms in front of the body; drawing the body *back* from you; an obvious shifting in the chair.

4. *The interviewer likes what you're saying.* Most of the time when the person you're talking to is leaning forward in the chair, it's a sign that you're being well received. Incidentally, this is something to remember yourself just in case your interviewer is a believer in body language.

The Informational Tug-of-War

An interesting informational tug-of-war frequently takes place in a job interview situation. The interviewer, especially in the first or second interview, is reluctant to tell you much about the company and its problems, the feeling being why should a lot of people who aren't going to get the job know about the company's internal problems? On the other hand, your chances of getting the job will increase the more aware you are of these problems and the more you can key your presentation to them.

So, there are two things to bear in mind here. First of all, don't interpret the reluctance of the interviewer to share with you a lot of details about the company as a sign that the company isn't interested in you. Accept the reluctance as part of the game. Second, when you ask questions (see next section), see if you can find out the answer indirectly. An example: "In my last job, I had to work especially hard at making sure that the three or four departments I was working with were communicating with each other. Do you think that might be a problem here?"

VII

Coming Out on Top in the Job Interview: Putting It All to Work

Talent does you no good, unless somebody else discovers it.

Enough rehearsing. Now it's time to go through the actual interview process.

It starts with the moment you make the appointment. To begin with, don't be in too much of a hurry to be the first person interviewed. A survey we ran showed that the first person interviewed for a job is three times *less* likely to be hired than the last person interviewed for the job. So, while first impressions are important, *last* impressions are probably more lasting.

Yet another survey we conducted turned up some interesting findings on how the day of the week and the time of day you show for an interview can affect your chances of being hired. Asked to name the "worst" day of the week for an interview, more than 50% of the top management and personnel executives named Monday (for obvious reasons, I would imagine, given the fact that Monday is usually the most pressured day of the week for many executives). The next "worst" day, according to our survey, was Friday. So, for what it's worth, your chances of being hired are probably better on a Tuesday, Wednesday or Thursday than on a Monday or Friday.

There are exceptions. If you're looking for a nonmanagerial position, for instance, it usually pays to be the first in line, so if you see an ad in Sunday's paper, be the first person at the company's office on Monday morning. And while it's true that Friday is not generally the best time to be interviewed, it's also true that most recruiters and agencies know of job openings on Friday that won't appear in the newspaper until the following Sunday. So, if you contact these recruiters or agencies on a Friday, you can sometimes get a head start.

As far as the *time* of day goes, our survey showed that the hour of day top management and personnel directors consider the "worst" time to interview is late afternoon (between 4 p.m. and 5 p.m.), with early morning (8 to 9:30) a reasonably close second. Here again, logic tells us why. During the early hours of the morning, most executives are preoccupied with what they have to accomplish the rest of the day, while late in the afternoon most people tend to be preoccupied with getting out of the office. And here again, there are exceptions. I know a financial executive who, during the period he was out of work, used to suggest breakfast interviews, as early as 7:30. "Even if the person who was supposed to interview me didn't want to get to work that early," the man explained to me, "the fact that I was ready for work at so early an hour told him that I was industrious."

And while I'm on the subject, let me tell you about my bad weather theory of interviews. Based on my experience, going to an interview when the weather is terrible gives you a better shot at getting hired than if the weather is nice. Why? For one thing, getting there in spite of the bad weather shows eagerness. Many interviewers (I know I do) will assume that if you braved the snow or rain or hail or sleet to come to the interview, you'll do the same when it comes to getting to work. Another thing, you probably won't have much competition on that bad, rainy day as you would on a nice day. The interviewer will be able to spend more time with you, which gives you more time to present your case. So remember, don't be a fair-weather candidate.

If your appointment is more than a week in advance, send a short note confirming the appointment. Let the interviewer know that you're looking forward to the meeting. It's a little thing, but it will make an impression.

I've already covered some of the general ideas of good

interview performance, so let me list here the points that deserve special mention.

First, a list of absolute no no's.

1. *Don't smoke*—even if the interviewer smokes or invites you to do so. One good reason is that if you're very nervous, you may have trouble lighting the cigarette. You might also get ashes on the rug, or, who knows, burn a hole in a chair.

2. *Don't drink alcohol*—even if it's at lunch and the interviewer is drinking. Years ago, we failed to place a high executive who was about to be hired because on the day he was being entertained at the country club where he was going to be supplied a membership, he took one more drink than the other executives. *One drink more!* Look at it this way. When you're on a job interview, you're working. Drinking dulls your wits, and your interview performance.

3. *Don't confuse ego with confidence*. Few things you do in an interview will hurt your chances more than turning the interview into an ego trip. Yes, you have to talk about yourself in an interview, and yes, you have to stress your accomplishments and exude confidence. But watch the sweeping "I" statements. Don't create the impression that if it hadn't been for you, your previous company would have gone bankrupt. Use "we" (in most instances) when you're talking about accomplishments on your last job. Be careful not to *repeat* the positive statements you say about yourself. And don't be afraid to plug into your conversation a fair number of "in my view," or "in my opinion's." Companies like people who are confident but deplore egotistical prima donnas.

4. *Don't name drop*. It's nice that you're on a first-name basis with a certain senator or celebrity, but don't mention it unless the subject comes up, and don't make a big deal about it. *Don't try to impress the people who interview you with the people you know*. In most cases, name dropping will only work against you.

5. *Don't get into an argument*. About *anything*: baseball, books, politics, philosophy. Resist the temptation to correct the interviewer if you feel the person is misinformed (unless, of course, the misconception is directly related to you). One

of the surest ways to lose the interview decision is to win an argument with the interviewer.

6. *Never chew gum.*

7. *Never take anybody else to the interview.* Not even your spouse. *Especially* not your spouse. If somebody comes with you, have them wait outside the building.

8. *Never make as a condition for taking a job the hiring of your spouse.* Well, almost never. If you're being offered a job in some remote place where your spouse may have trouble finding work, this condition might not be out of line.

9. *Never ask to use the interviewer's phone.* If you have to make a call, ask the receptionist.

10. *Never tell jokes.* It's good to show a sense of humor in an interview, but interviews aren't the place to tell jokes. I think I have a pretty good sense of humor, but not once in more than thirty years has a job candidate made me laugh with a joke.

11. *Don't carry anything but your briefcase or purse into the interviewer's office.* Leave your coat and any packages you may have with you in the reception area.

12. *Don't use jargon.* Talk the interviewer's language, which is basic English. Watch the ''You know,'' ''I mean's,'' and the overuse of certain adjectives: ''fantastic,'' ''super,'' ''fabulous,'' and so on. And don't get into what some people call ''psychobabble,'' in which you talk about your ''space,'' what you're ''into,'' and how you couldn't get your ''head together'' on your last job.

So much for what you shouldn't do. Now let's turn to some reminders on the positive side.

1. *Look and feel your best.* We've already discussed appearance (Chapter III), so I won't go into the subject in detail except to emphasize again that you *must* look as good as you're capable of looking when you go into any interview. If you're a man with a heavy beard and your interview is in the afternoon, have a razor with you so you can shave just before the interview. Have a freshly pressed shirt with you as well. In the event you're not feeling yourself—you have a really bad cold, etc.—see if you can cancel the interview, but only

when you're convinced your appearance or condition may work against you.

2. *Get there on time.* Obvious? You bet—and for the best of reasons. Our surveys show that showing up late for a job interview will probably hurt your chances of being hired in roughly 70 percent of the interviews you go on, and will definitely hurt your chances in nearly 50 percent of the interviews.

Give yourself at least a half-hour margin. Don't show up at the office a half hour early, but make sure you're at the building or the site. If you're early, you'll avoid the tension that invariably arises when you're running late—and don't underestimate the ability of this tension to hurt you at the interview. Use the waiting time for some useful purpose. If you're driving, do some paperwork in the parking lot. Read. Go over your notes for the interview.

If the interview site is somewhere you've never been before, and you're not sure of the directions, make a dry run the day before—a precaution against finding yourself in that horrible position of being lost five minutes before a scheduled appointment. And in the event that you know ahead of time you're going to arrive late (I consider anything over five minutes past your scheduled time "late"), you're probably better off calling to cancel the interview than arriving late and flustered.

3. *Pay scrupulous attention to etiquette.* It starts the minute you enter the reception area—with a smile and a friendly hello to the receptionist, and a thank you when you've been announced. Show the same courtesy to the secretary who escorts you into the interviewer's office. Unless you're invited to do otherwise, refer to the interviewer as "Mr." or "Mrs." or "Ms." A usually reliable way of seeing just how familiar the interviewer wants you to be is the manner in which he or she introduces his or her own name to you. If the person uses a nickname or a shortened first name, "Hi, I'm Pat Evans," and calls you by your first name, you can do the same. When in doubt, be formal and use the last name. Sometimes, you can get a clue from how the secretary intro-

duces you. If the secretary says, "Mr." or "Mrs.", follow suit.

4. *Be observant.* As soon as you walk into the interviewer's office, look around for possible conversation points—things that the two of you may have in common. Are there photographs on the desk of children who look to be the same age as your own? Are there photographs on the wall that show your interviewer has the same athletic interests you have? Are there any trophies around? Check out any books lying on the desk. Maybe you've just finished the same book. Look at the view: is it special? Are there any unusual pieces of furniture in the room? Anything you can mention or bring up that will get the two of you *sharing* information, showing mutual enthusiasm, will make the rest of the interview go much more smoothly. I know a salesman who has a marvelous eye for clothing. You should see the response he gets from people when he says how much he admires a jacket or a suit, and then proceeds to name the designer. Not a bad tactic.

5. *Show the appropriate attitude.* Let's start out with what's *inappropriate*. It's inappropriate to be patronizing or intimidating to a lower-level person, regardless of how much older than that individual you may be, and regardless of how much more money you were making than that person in your last job. Respect the fact that the personnel interviewer has a job to do and may be intimidated by you anyway. Respect the fact that this person, no matter how much less intelligent he or she may seem, has the power to move you along in the interview process or to scotch your chances for the job. And remember that truly important people don't have to act important.

It's inappropriate to try to impress an interviewer—particularly an interviewer who may not be familiar with your particular specialty—with the scope of your technical knowledge. Avoid jargon that has meaning to you and the people in your field, and nobody else. Keep your conversation as non-technical as possible, except in those cases when the interviewer shares your technical knowledge.

It's inappropriate to try to pressure the person interviewing you into offering you the job. ("Mr. Adams, I have several excellent offers pending, so you're going to have to make your mind up about me very soon.'') Of course, if you *do* have several excellent offers pending and you're prepared to take the calculated risk that mentioning these offers won't offend the interviewer, go ahead and mention them. But do it in a matter-of-fact way; don't present the information in the form of an ultimatum.

Now for the *appropriate* attitude.

Obviously, you want your attitude to be businesslike but at the same time warm and courteous. And, above all, make sure that everybody you come into contact with (the receptionist, the secretary, the interviewer) senses from you a feeling that you consider them important.

The way you convey this is to recognize that each person, in his or her own way, *is* important. Suppose you were waiting on line in the motor vehicle bureau to have your car registered. You've waited a half hour, only to find that you made a minor mistake on the application—a mistake that has just been pointed out by the person behind the counter.

You could, of course, make a big fuss—complain that you're going to call the supervisor. Or, you can acknowledge the importance of the person behind the counter and direct your strategy accordingly. ''I know you must be busy, but is there a way we can handle this that doesn't involve my going to the back of the line?''

Which approach do you think will produce the best results?

Respect the time and the importance of *all* the people you meet during the course of job hunting, and you will be surprised at the respect and cooperation you get in return.

6. *Be enthusiastic*. Keep in mind our survey findings. *As many as 90 percent of the interviewers you're likely to run into consider basic enthusiasm a very important qualification for being hired*. Smile. Be responsive. Radiate energy.

7. *Know ahead of time the points you want to emphasize, and make sure you emphasize them*. Before you go into any interview, you should always have an idea which of the ''selling points'' about yourself you feel need stressing the most in this particular interview and for this particular job. Choose three or four (no more), and make sure that you keep

hitting hard on these factors throughout the interview, albeit in different ways, of course. Let's say that you've picked the following three points:

1. Your strong background in the industry
2. Your contacts in the field
3. Your skill at motivating your subordinates

Keep in mind that these may not be your strongest features as a candidate, all in all, but for this particular job they seem highly relevant. It may well be, as you navigate the interview, that your assessment changes, and you want to add a new point: Your willingness to do *more* than is expected of you. No matter. By having a plan, you give a structure to your presentation. At the first opportunity, mention the factors you've decided to stress ahead of time and don't be shy about referring back to them. ("As I mentioned earlier, I've been in the business a long time and I know most of the people in it . . .")

What I'm suggesting here, really, is that you *custom design every interview*. Get a game plan. Know ahead of time what you want to accomplish in the interview, and make it your business to achieve it.

8. *Make sure the conversation goes two ways*. Which means that neither you nor the interviewer does the bulk of the talking. Keep your answers brief. Stick to the subject, and don't get sidetracked by stories or discussions that don't relate to the job. If your interviewer likes to talk, don't interfere, but make sure you have enough time to get across the points you want to emphasize about yourself.

9. *Don't be shy about asking for a chance*. Not *begging* for a chance, asking for one. For instance, if it appears in the course of an interview that the interviewer is concerned about your qualifications, I see nothing wrong at all in offering to do a project, without a fee. If you're a copywriter, ask if you can work on a project or two. If you're looking for a job in research, offer to do a brief assignment. Chances are, they won't take you up on your offer, but the fact that you made it will inspire confidence in you. If they offer you the chance,

all the better: you're halfway home to getting the job. Of course, make sure when you make this offer that you can deliver.

A business friend of mine named Arthur, looking for a financial analyst, called me. Arthur was associated with one of the giant corporations. He was holding interviews in his hotel suite one day when there was a sudden downpour of rain late in the afternoon. My candidate showed up on time, but drenched to the skin. Arthur suggested that the candidate take off his jacket, but his shirt was wet as well. Arthur then suggested that the candidate remove his shirt. Eventually the candidate was being interviewed in his undershorts. During the course of the interview, Arthur looked at his watch and commented that he hadn't been to church that day. The candidate said he would be glad to go with him to the church. So he put on his soggy clothes. He covered his head with a newspaper, and ran with Arthur to the church a block away. "When I got inside the church and kneeled," Arthur described, "I noticed that the guy was just sitting there, so I asked him why he wasn't kneeling."

"Because I'm not Catholic," the candidate said.

"Then how come you're in church?" Arthur asked.

"Because I really want this job," the candidate said.

"You're hired," my friend said.

10. *Show a willingness to do something extra.* A friend of mine who is the president of a small consulting company hired an executive secretary recently mainly because the woman indicated, during the interview, that she was very good at making travel arrangements. "I imagine you do a good deal of traveling," she said. "I've done a lot of work with airlines, and I know the ins and outs of the best fare deals. I think I could save you money on airfares." The lesson here is this: If you can show the interviewer that you can handle not only everything that's required in the job, but *more* to boot, you give yourself that much of an edge over the competition.

11. *Have a small notebook and pen with you.* A little thing, but it could come in very handy if you're looking for names and numbers. I always liked it when a candidate would

take out a small notebook and pen to jot down a name I was giving. It showed a sense of organization.

12. *Come away from the interview with something.* If you sense that the particular job for which you're being interviewed isn't suitable for you, don't consider the interview a lost cause. See if you can't get some suggestions from the interviewer—a lead or two for other jobs. And here's something else to remember: if the person in your first interview tells you that he or she wants to send you along for a second interview, see what you can find out about the second person. What's that person like? Where did he or she go to school? Does he or she have any hobbies? sail? play golf? Does the first interviewer have any suggestions as to how you might make a more favorable impression on this second person?

When It's Your Turn to Ask the Questions

At some point in the interview, usually toward the end, the interviewer is going to ask you if you have any questions. This invitation is more than a formality, so don't neglect the opportunity. Our surveys show that as many as 90 percent of the executives who interview candidates expect you to ask questions. The chance to do so gives you time to find out things about the company that could help you decide to accept the offer, should you get it. It also gives you a chance to impress your interviewer with what you have to bring to the position.

This session of the interview is not—repeat *not*—the time to discuss the mechanics of the job. Don't ask about salary or benefits or office location. You can always discuss these things after the offer comes through. Instead, ask questions that suggest that, while you're confident you can do the job, you have some reservations that might affect your decision to accept it or not. Here are six such questions. If you can, ask any two or three of them.

1. I'm curious to know why you've gone outside the company to fill this position?

2. What were the strengths and weaknesses of the person whose place I'm taking?
3. Assuming I'm offered the job and take it, what sort of performance is the company expecting?
4. How receptive is the company to new ideas?
5. What would you say is the number one priority for the person who takes this job?
6. What would you say are the main strengths a person who gets this job needs to have?

Wrapping Up the Interview in Your Favor

Never expect to walk out of an interview with an offer in your pocket. No matter how much you've impressed the interviewer, he or she is going to want time to think the matter over and to talk it over with others. So don't pressure the interviewer into making a decision before he's ready to make this decision. Your pressure could backfire.

End the interview on a positive note. Tell the interviewer that you're more interested and excited about the job now than ever before. Let it be known—without pleading—that you want the job. At some point, say the five words that almost every interviewer will respond to: *"I won't let you down."* Thank the interviewer for his or her time. Say how much you've enjoyed the talk, and how profitable you've found the interview.

If you're feeling confident, try the following tactic. Tell the interviewer (before he or she gets a chance to say it to you) that you imagine they'll want to take a few days to make the decision, which is good because you want a few days too. Then offer to call him or her and ask whether a certain date is okay. You may get the familiar "Don't call us, we'll call you." Then again, the interviewer may take you up on your offer. Or, the interviewer may tell you to call sometime next week.

Apply *gentle* pressure. You want to nudge an offer out of the company, not force one.

Counteracting "Stress" Techniques

"Stress" interviewing techniques—things that interviewers do deliberately to upset you so they can see how you respond to stress—have gotten a lot of play in books and articles on job hunting. But this is more because they're fascinating to read about than because they happen with any great frequency. I've known a few executive who had tricks they would sometimes use to get a candidate riled. However, most of the interviewers you're likely to meet are going to play it straight with you. They're busy; they don't have time for games.

Even so, it doesn't hurt to be prepared for that small minority of interviewers who may try, in different ways, to intimidate you. Here are some of the most common stress techniques, and the best ways to counteract them:

1. *Purposely sitting you so that the sun is in your eyes*. Subjecting you to glare is one of the oldest stress interviewing techniques known to man (police sometimes use the technique when they're interrogating suspects). Should a chair you are invited to sit in subject you to any amount of glare, ask the interviewer right away if you may move. The interviewer won't give you any problem and will probably be impressed with your common sense.

2. *Sitting you in a chair that is slightly off balance*. The idea behind this tactic is to keep you mildly unsettled throughout the interview, but sometimes the interviewer is simply curious to see how you'll respond. The best counteraction is to ask the interviewer casually if it's okay to sit in another chair. If there is no other chair in the room, tilt your weight in such a way that the chair won't rock. Never ask the interviewer to bring in another chair: the disruption won't help your chances.

3. *Interrupting the interview with frequent—or lengthy— phone conversations*. The main thing here is to conceal your irritation. If a phone call seems to be going on endlessly, look

around the room for a stockholder's report, a business magazine, or any other literature about the company. If there's a newspaper on the executive's desk, you might point to it to see if the interviewer minds you're reading it. Show the interviewer you don't like to waste time. Obviously, you should never remove any papers from the executive desk. If you sense that the phone conversation is getting personal, take a different seat further away from the interviewer's desk.

4. *Offering you something to eat—but without a plate*. You're sitting at a coffee table in the interviewer's office. Somebody brings out a piece of sponge cake, a danish, perhaps, but with no plate to handle the thing properly. This is an easy technique to respond to: you simply say, "No, thank you."

5. *The group interview*. Instead of one person firing questions at you, there are three or four, or as many as six. Pay attention to all of them (making sure that you glance at each one every so often), but concentrate most of your attention on the person you figure to be the most important decision maker in the crowd. When you're asked a question, direct your answer to the person who asked the question—not to the group.

6. *Having you interviewed by your would-be subordinate*. It doesn't happen very often, but it *does* happen. Not wanting to upset a staff person, a company will actually have that person interview the would-be boss. Play along. Keep in mind that all your subordinate wants, really, is a fair boss— somebody who knows the field, somebody who is pleasant.

7. *Keeping you waiting*. It happens. Sometimes unavoidably and sometimes because the interviewer is inconsiderate. My rule of thumb has always been this: if you have another interview scheduled, or if you have to get back to your office, you don't wait around more than fifteen minutes past your scheduled appointment. You speak to the secretary, explain

your problem, and try to make arrangements for another interview. Most executives will understand and won't give you a hard time.

8. *The silent treatment.* Occasionally you run into an interviewer who, somewhere in the middle of the interview, suddenly clams up. This is a common interviewing technique known, appropriately enough, as the "silent treatment." The idea is to catch you off guard, to trick you into dropping your mask. Frequently it works. Silence is threatening to a lot of people, who often respond to it with loose talk and nonsense. People say things that are often irrelevant—and sometimes damaging to their chances.

The best way to handle the silent treatment is to prepare for it ahead of time. *Expect* it to happen, even though it won't most of the time. Be prepared with something pertinent or interesting to say—an addendum, perhaps, to a point you've made earlier. ("You know, something just struck me about what we were talking about earlier—the question of motivating people . . .") Give the subject, whatever it is, a minute or two, pause, then ask the interviewer: "Would you like me to go on?"

Another good response is to have a question or two ready at all times. If the silence continues, ask the interviewer if he or she has any more questions for you. You might even *suggest* a question. ("Would you like to hear about the volunteer work I'm doing?")

The basic idea in dealing with the silent treatment, when it comes, is to use it to your advantage. See it as an opportunity, not a threat.

There's one type of stress interview I haven't mentioned because it doesn't fit into quite the same category but can still cause you stress. I'm talking about a situation in which the interviewer who would be your boss is obnoxiously rude. This won't happen very often, but my feeling is that if that person can't show simple courtesy at an interview, he or she isn't working for a company that I'd be very happy at. Trust your instincts, and if you think you're being unnecessarily abused, make a quick but polite exit. On the other hand, if this is your first interview, play it cool. One rude interviewer isn't necessarily a reflection of the rest of the company.

Personality Testing

Time was in the mid- to late 1950s that many companies were big on giving their prospective employees personality tests the better to determine the psychological fitness of the people coming to work for them. Not as many firms use these tests any more, and for the best of reasons: they weren't particularly effective. As a psychologist friend of mine once explained to me: "The only thing that personality tests showed us was which of the people were intelligent enough to answer the questions in the way they figured we wanted them answered."

In the event that you're asked to take personality tests, don't make an issue. If you want the job, take them. It's unlikely that your performance on the test will mean all that much in the final counting; but refusing to take the test could ruin your chances before you even get a chance to prove yourself in an interview.

Finding Out How Well You Did

As soon as you can after the interview, find a place where you can sit down by yourself and go over in your mind how well you did, concentrating, however, on what went *wrong*. I know, it's hard to be objective, but here's a little test you can give yourself after each interview. Simply rate how well you think you did in each of the areas mentioned in the question from 1 to 10, with 10 being the highest score.

1. Did I look as good as I'm capable of looking?
2. Was I as informed about the company as I should have been?
3. Was I relaxed and in control of myself?
4. Did I answer the questions in a way that stressed the three most important things: my ability, my willingness, and my suitability?

5. Did I *listen* to the interviewer?
6. Did I steer questions toward the points I wanted to stress?
7. Was I observant enough?
8. Did the interviewer get interested and involved in what I was saying?
9. Did I tailor my answers to the type of interviewer I was interviewed by.
10. Did I present an accurate and favorable picture of myself?

Send a Follow-Up Letter

No matter how the interview went, or where the two of you left the matter when you said goodbye, you should send off a brief letter to the interviewer the same night or, at the latest, the day after. Keep it simple. Thank the interviewer for his or her time. Express your enthusiasm and interest, and try to sneak a line or two of "swell" into the letter as well. Here's a good example:

Dear Ms. Fields:

Just a brief note to thank you for taking the time to talk with me today about the public relations position you're looking to fill. I enjoyed your talk and found your comments very helpful.

As I told you during the interview, I'd like the chance to show how well I could handle the job (I'm more convinced now that we've spoken that it's a job I could do well), and I'd be delighted to discuss the matter further with you at your convenience.

I look forward to hearing from you. Thanks again for your time and encouragement.

Sincerely,

Send thank-you notes not only for the first interview in a job situation but each time you meet and are interviewed by somebody new. I've known candidates who've even written thank-you notes to secretaries who've been helpful. It all adds up.

Going Beyond the Thank-You Letter

Okay, you've been interviewed. You like the company, the job, the people, but you're not sure how they like you. Here's a suggestion that most of your competition won't follow, but it can have a powerful impact on the people considering you.

After the interview, prepare a brief report—a memo, really—on what you might do, if requested, to solve a problem the company has that relates to your potential job with the company.

This report could be one page, or it could be ten pages. It doesn't have to be definitive. You can "blue-sky" since nobody expects you to know the ins and outs of the company's problems anyway. Write a covering letter with the report so that the company knows you're simply taking a "shot." Let them know that your only purpose in this report is to show them how your mind works. Underplay the tone. Make sure you emphasize that these are things that you "might" do, not things that should be done. Suggest, don't order.

Special Interviewing Considerations

The advice I've offered throughout this chapter should serve you well in most situations, but there are a few special situations that warrant mention. These have to do with some specific feature that could work against you if you don't know how to defuse it.

Making Age Work for You

When does being "too old" become a handicap in the job market, and equally, when does being "too young" become a handicap? Good questions, both, but not questions that you can answer easily or quickly. Age discrimination, of course, is illegal. But how are you going to make a case that the only reason you weren't hired for a particular job was your age?

This may sound silly, but there are certain advantages to being one of the oldest candidates to apply for a particular job, and advantages, too, to being the youngest candidate. What it comes down to is how successfully you're able to press the advantage.

Let's start with being on the shady side of fifty. The older you are, the more experienced you are—not just in job skills but in life skills. You're settled. You know what life is all about. Your earning requirements are stable since, chances are, your children have already grown. You respect a job, and you earn that respect (you come from a generation, remember, where the work ethic really meant something). You are steady and reliable. You can be counted on.

To sum up, you're a darn good employee. In some way, your way—at the interview, in your résumé—you have to make sure the people who are considering you understand this. Don't *evade* the age issue, in other words. Capitalize on it.

Recently, I gave a speech before a national group of accountants involved in data processing administration. I mentioned in my talk that the computer field is relatively a new field, and as a result was populated mostly by young people. Even so, computer programmers are hard to find. I pointed out that there's a big market of competent people out there, ready to be trained, who are older than the average. The guest speaker at the luncheon that followed my morning session was the Executive Vice-President of Finance with one of the multi-billion dollar industrials. During his prepared speech, he managed to include one comment which I will not forget: "If I got nothing else out of this conference but Mr. Half's suggestion to train older people for computer departments in order to get competency along with stability, the meeting was well worth while."

Appearance is probably more important the older you are, but this doesn't mean you should go out of your way to look younger. Look your age, but look healthy and vibrant. Radiate energy. It won't work all the time. You may often find yourself in an interview where the company appears to want a younger person. Accept it; but remember, too, that there are just as many companies where age *won't* make a difference.

But don't take anything for granted. Here are a few of the things you can expect to be going on in the mind of the interviewer if you're considerably older than the other candidates, and the best ways to overcome them:

1. *Is this person's health going to be a problem?* If you're in good health, let it be known at some time in the interview that you have a fine attendance record. Maybe you have a ninety-two-year-old grandmother who still does her own gardening. Mention her.

2. *Is this person too set in his (her) ways to adapt to our system?* A legitimate concern, since there is a tendency among some people as they grow older to become a little less receptive to innovation. On the other hand, innovation that's blessed with an overlay of experience is a terrific combination. So show an interest in new ideas.

3. *Can this person get along with a younger boss?* Another legitimate concern, but one that's easily defused. Don't talk about age, either directly or indirectly. Don't say things like: "When I was your age . . ." or, "Back when I was starting out in 1940 . . ." As far as you're concerned, age is not an issue.

Let Being Young Work for You, Too

Okay, you don't have any experience, but nobody expects you to have much experience when you're younger. What you're expected to have when you're younger is energy, enthusiasm, ambition, curiosity, and a willingness to learn.

The most important quality you can convey in an interview when you're just out of college or high school is a strong desire to work hard. Don't be afraid to let people know that you're ambitious, but don't give the impression that you're in all that much of a hurry to succeed. Let the interviewer know that you realize nobody is going to hand you advancement—you're going to have to work for it and earn it. That's fine with you.

Go heavy on your school experience. Did you work on the school paper? Were you treasurer of a fund-raising committee? Were you in honor societies? None of these things may seem to mean much to you in terms of the job you're applying for, but they will help set you apart from the rest of the crowd. If you've had summer jobs, mention them. They show ambition. If you've sold things, mention that, too.

Above all, don't work so hard at appearing mature and knowing that you create the impression you know all there is to do. Ask questions. Seek advice. It is much better, if you're very young and looking for a job, to appear unsure of yourself than to appear smug. You can teach people how to handle a job, but you can't teach somebody not to be smug.

One final word about age. Somebody once asked George Burns why he thought they'd asked him to play the part of God in the movie *Oh, God.* "Because," Burns said, "they couldn't find an older actor." Never apologize for how old you are. Take advantage of it.

For Women Only

If I were writing this book ten years ago, I would have included a special chapter on women. But these days, the number of considerations that deserve special attention from women is relatively small. What's true in the main for men looking for jobs is equally true for women. I'm not saying that as a woman you're not going to run into situations in which your sex is going to work against your chances; but consider the facts. A survey we conducted not long ago showed that when a woman and a man are competing for the same job in the $15,000 to $50,000 a year bracket, everything else being reasonably equal, the job will go more frequently to the woman. The reason is that many companies are going out of their way to recruit talented and able women.

Probably the biggest problem a woman candidate faces that a man doesn't has to do with marriage and family. Nobody ever thinks twice about hiring a man who may be contemplating marriage or whose wife may be having a baby. But some companies, for obvious reasons, may be reluctant to invest a lot of money to train a woman who may decide within a year or so that she'd be much happier working at home as a full-time mother. Some companies, too, will be concerned that you are married to a man who may have to relocate as part of *his* career development. (Although, interestingly enough, the reverse is now beginning to take place: husbands having to change jobs because the wife wants to relocate for a better career opportunity.)

So anything you can do to reinforce the notion that your domestic situation will in no way interfere with your responsibilities to the company is going to work in your favor. Here are some of the questions the interviewer may be *thinking* about, whether or not the questions get asked, and what you might do to defuse that apprehension.

1. *Is she going to get pregnant and have to leave the job for three or four months?* Agreed, it's none of the interviewer's business. But if your plans are definitely not to have any children—for a long while, at least—it doesn't hurt to volunteer this information, albeit in an indirect way. Such as, "I'm very serious about my career. My husband understands this, and is very supportive."

2. *She has young children: will they interfere with her duties at work?* Chances are, you've made adequate arrangements for your children. Otherwise, you wouldn't be looking for a job. Stress at some point in the interview how lucky you are to have somebody (whoever that is) who loves your children, whom your children love, and so on.

3. *She's single now, but what's going to happen after she gets married?* The same principle as in the first question. "Career" is a code word. If you stress it, it will convey the

notion that your mind is on business, and marriage won't interfere with your career.

4. *Can she handle the pressure?* Women have proved themselves in the marketplace today, and I don't think you have to worry too much about this question. Time was when some placement specialists would tell a woman to, in effect, "act like a man," whatever that means. Nonsense. Be businesslike, and be yourself. You have nothing more to prove to the interviewer than a man does.

VIII

What to Do Once the Offer Comes In

The better choice than either is sometimes neither.

Years back, there was a movie starring Robert Redford called *The Candidate*. Redford played a young idealist who is induced by a seasoned and jaded political campaigner to run for senator. The young candidate pulls a major upset and wins the election. But in the movie's last scene, as he is being driven to the victory celebration, the candidate turns to the campaign manager and says: "*Now,* what do I do?"

Throughout this book, I've been telling you how to get hired. Now it's time to think about what you do when you've won the ultimate prize in the job search game: the job offer. In some respects, of course, you can relax. The pressure's off. But don't relax too much. You still have some work to do. You've got to weigh the offer to make sure you're making the right move. And once you've made up your mind, you then have to negotiate an arrangement that makes *you* happy and gets you and your employer off on the right track together.

It sounds easier than it is.

How Solid Is the Offer?

I've seen it hundreds of times: wishful thinking interfering with good judgment. "I've been offered a job," someone will tell me. "Great," I say. "When do you start?" "Well," they say, "I'm not really sure." "Is the money good?" I ask. "Well," they say, "we haven't really talked money. The fact is, they haven't really *offered* me the job yet—not officially anyway. But it's in the bag."

Sure it is! Make sure the offer you get is an *offer*. An offer means that someone has said to you: "We want you for this job. When can you start?" An offer isn't any of the following:

"We like the way you look."

"We think you could do well here."

"We're *very* interested in you."

"You're the front runner. It looks good."

I've known candidates who, on the basis of these statements, have retired from the job search game. They avoid other interviews. They give notice. I've known a few people who've celebrated the new "offer" by going on vacation. Then, whammo, they get back, make a call, and are told, politely, that something went wrong. A misunderstanding. "I'm very sorry. Somebody else came along who looked a little better than you. Of course, we'll keep your résumé on file."

So, beware the non-offer offer.

Do You Really Want the Job?

Nobody can answer this question but you, and your answer, of course, will depend upon any number of considerations, not the least of which is how badly you need the job.

If you've been following the guidelines set down for you in earlier chapters, you should have a pretty good idea of how much you really want a particular job *before* the offer is made. This isn't to say that you've absolutely made up your mind (being offered a job can sometimes make that job seem more attractive or less attractive to you, depending on your state of mind and state of finances). But you should be aware of how closely this job meets your needs and wants.

If you're convinced that the job being offered you is the right one for you at this time, don't agonize over a decision. Concentrate, instead, on negotiating the best possible terms. And even if the job is lacking in certain respects, don't be in a hurry to turn it down, especially if you're out of work.

To repeat, nobody but you can make the decision whether or not to take a job that's been offered you. But here are three questions you should be asking yourself in order to help you make the decision that's best for you.

1. *How badly do you need a job?* There is a point in every job search campaign—and it varies from person to person—when common sense dictates that you take any job you're offered that comes even close to the things you're looking for. In most instances, the main consideration is financial: how quickly you're sinking. In the event that finances are becoming a serious problem—serious enough, for instance, that they're causing tension in your home and making you lose sleep at night—don't be cavalier. Ignore the negatives in the job. See it as an opportunity to stabilize yourself. Recognize the reality of your situation. Subordinate your reservations about the job to the priorities of your present situation.

On the other hand, if you're currently working in a job that's paying you enough to live on and isn't causing you grief, don't accept the new job simply for the sake of a change. The beauty of looking for a job while you're already working, remember, is that it affords you the luxury of being independent and choosy. *Do not feel an obligation to take any job simply because it has been offered to you.* People turn down job offers all the time. But make sure you think through all the possibilities. Try to project ahead. Ask yourself if perhaps three or four months down the road, you might not regret your decision to turn the job down.

2. *How does this job fit into your long-term career picture?* I mentioned in the first chapter that my purpose in writing this book isn't to guide you in your career choices but to help you get hired. But now that you're considering a job offer, it might be a good time to offer a few comments. By and large, the most successful top executives are those men and women who had a clear and well-thought-out idea of what their long-term goals were, and who made each career decision not only on the strength of what a job may have offered in the way of money or responsibility at a particular time, but how that job fit into their long-term plans. It is easier than you think to get sidetracked: to lose sight of

what's going to bring you satisfaction in the long run because a job suddenly offers you the prospect of making considerably more money than you're making now.

I'm not saying discount the importance of money. Hardly. But as difficult as it is, try to weigh the short-term advantages of taking a job that offers you a sizeable jump in pay against the long-term advantages of pursuing a career plan that offers you a somewhat surer if longer route to long-term career goals.

Weigh the offer, yes. But use it, too, as an opportunity to examine what you want to do with your life and career. Project five years down the road, both in your present job, if you're still working, and in the job you've just been offered. Write down on a sheet of paper the various things you like about your current job and the things you don't like. Then make up a similar list (projecting, of course) for the job you've been offered. All I'm asking, really, is that you view your situation as objectively as you can.

Disregard the understandable excitement you feel as a result of the new offer. Forget the ego boost. Do your best to see yourself in the job you've been offered—not the exciting and romantic parts, but the pressure and the drudgery of it. If you can imagine yourself handling the *worst* that the job has to offer, and you still think you'll like it, you've done all a reasonable person can do in the way of answering the basic question of how happy you're going to be in that job.

3. *Are you and the company on the same wavelength?* Let's call it chemistry—the feeling you get when you walk into the company's offices. Is the place friendly enough for you? Is the company's philosophy of doing business one you can comfortably live with? You know yourself and your attitude toward work. How much will you have to alter it in order to fit into the company's mold?

Checking Up on the Company

Let's assume you're not so desperate that you're forced to take just about any reasonable job that's offered you. Let's also assume you've been offered a job that seems to offer you what you want, but you want to be fairly certain that you're making the right move. In this case, I say do unto the company that gave you the offer what the company did unto you: find out as much as you can about them. As long as you don't take too much time doing it, and as long as you're not unpleasant about it, most employers won't mind a little probing on your part. And if they *do* mind it, you probably have reason to be suspicious.

Here's how to set about it:

1. *The interview revisited.* The first step is to call the person who made the offer. Say how delighted about the offer you are and ask if the two of you can meet again to talk about the job. You shouldn't run into any resistance.

This time when you go to the interview, keep an eye open for cues you may have missed in your previous visits. Chat with the receptionist. Ask casually how long the receptionist has been with the firm. You might ask off-handedly what sort of a person the department head (your would-be boss) is to work for. You could find out from this little discussion that the firm is a revolving door.

At the meeting itself, start out with basic questions, about pension and benefits, but eventually ask the person you're speaking with to describe for you some of the problems that your predecessor may have had in the job. In the event that the person who had your job is still with the company (perhaps he or she has been promoted), see if you can sit down and talk with this person.

2. *Where's the company heading?* Assuming you haven't already done so in preparing for the interview, learn as much as you can about the company's financial position. If it's a public company, get its annual and interim reports. If it's a private company, find out who its banker is and the partner in charge of the company audit at its CPA firm. (I'm assuming here that you're being hired for a middle- or senior-level management position. If you're being hired for a lower-level

position and you start asking these kinds of questions, you'll look foolish.)

Be low-key. Impress upon your would-be employers that your current position is not desperate, and that you want to feel secure about this offer. If your efforts to get this kind of information run into a stone wall, try at least to get a business plan out of them. These plans tend to be overly optimistic, but you'll have an idea about the projected return on investment and the owner's expansion program.

Don't take the company's financial condition for granted. There is a direct correlation between the financial condition of the company and the opportunities for your advancement in that company. The smaller the profits, the fewer the chances for promotions and raises. But with one exception. Sometimes you may have a chance to work for a company that is in a turnaround situation. If the company is indeed on the rebound and you're along for the ride, you're in great shape. But it's a gamble, so take note of the odds. If you have a family, you may not want to run the necessary risk.

3. *Getting in on the right track.* You'll never really get to know the political nature of a company until you've worked for them for a few months, but it's always good to be hired by somebody who is in a secure and powerful position, and not somebody on the way out. How do you tell? Well, you may have to do some digging. Talk to your colleagues. See how your boss is regarded in the industry. Maybe you have a contact in a competing firm. I'm constantly amazed at how much competing firms know about each other.

Of course, if the person who hires you *does* happen to be on the wrong side of a company power struggle, you could always ask for a transfer, once you get a clearer picture of the office political scene. So don't let the relatively tenuous position of your would-be boss be the only consideration.

4. *Where do you go from there?* Each company has its own distinctive career pattern, and you should make it your business to find out whether the executives in the department you're about to work for have a reasonable shot at top

management. Read the literature the firm puts out about itself. See if you can get the biographies of the firm's top management people. See how many of the officers came out of your own field.

And Now for the Money

First things first. Do everything in your power—and sometimes, I grant you, it's impossible—to keep money out of any discussions you're having with your prospective employers until *after* they've made you an offer. Remember, though, an offer is not truly an offer unless the salary has been settled.

Chances are that what you're expecting and what they're prepared to pay in salary and benefits are not far apart, for, as we discussed in Chapter III, the amount of salary you can expect will be determined, to a large extent, by two factors: (1) what the company is accustomed to paying in this particular position; and (2) what your previous salary was. In any event, keep in mind the cardinal rule of negotiating salary for a new job: wait for the offer before you start talking money.

A corollary to this rule is to withhold your final decision until the money issue is settled. The person who offers you the job might say: "I don't see any problem when it comes to salary, so what do you say: are you coming aboard?", and expect you to answer immediately. But as soon as you make a commitment, you lose leverage. Don't play it *too* coy, though. If you want the job, tell the person or people you're dealing with that you're delighted with the offer, you're anxious to settle as soon as possible, and that all that remains to be done is to iron out some of the financial details. Make the acceptance *contingent,* in other words, on a satisfactory salary arrangement. "I'm ready to start," you might say, "as soon as we get together on salary."

The Basics of Negotiating

The basic principles of negotiation are the same whether you're buying a house, haggling with a merchant at a foreign bazaar, or talking to your prospective employers about money. Three principles eclipse all the rest in their importance:

1. You have to know ahead of time the market value for whatever it is you're negotiating.

2. You have to know ahead of time what you *want* and what you're willing to settle for.

3. You have to get the other party to make the opening offer.

In every negotiation, regardless of what's been discussed, there is a point beyond which further discussion can't take place. Somebody who wants to sell a house for $175,000 may entertain an offer of $165,000. Offer $125,000, and you will probably insult the person. A fundamental understanding in any negotiation is that the parties are negotiating in good faith.

As a general rule, you should try to get a salary that is at least 10 to 20 percent higher than the salary of your previous jobs. There are two prime exceptions: first, if you're changing careers; and second, if you've been out of work for several months and have no reasonable prospects.

When you're asked how much money you'd like, it's always a good idea to say what you've been accustomed to and what you're looking for ("in the neighborhood of" is a good way to put it), rather than what you *need* to live on. Try always to talk money in terms of what the job and the responsibility are "worth," and not so much in terms of what you'd like to be paid. You may get a lower offer. How you handle that counter offer should be determined by how much *below* your original demand the offer was. You've given a figure that represents what you think you're worth. So even if you get the employer to raise the offer midway between your demand and their offer, you're still settling for *less*. Here are some options:

1. *Ask about perks*. Okay, the company can't meet your salary demands. But maybe they can provide you with a car, or a larger expense account. Get together with your accountant: see if you can arrange for benefits that could help you save on taxes.

2. *Get a commitment for a raise once you've proven your-self.* I prefer this approach in most situations. "Okay," you say. "I'm not going to argue salary with you. I want the job, but the money isn't right, so I'll tell you what we can do. I'll start at the salary you mentioned, but in three months, you'll have the option either to fire me for not living up to what I said I could do, or else to give me the money I feel I'm worth."

3. *Offer to work for nothing.* This is a bolder version of the last suggestion. Chances are, nobody is going to take you up on it, but it may be worth a try. You should try this if the two of you are very far apart. "I tell you what," you might say. "I really can't work for the salary you're offering. But let's try this. I'll work for you for free for two weeks. If, after that two weeks, you don't think I'm worth the money I'm asking, you can fire me. Otherwise, hire me at the salary I think I'm worth."

4. *Negotiate a different title.* Or more responsibility that might lead to quicker advancement.

Giving Notice and Dealing with a Counter Offer

You've received a job offer and you've pretty much agreed upon the particulars. Now you go back to the company you're currently working for (assuming you're employed) and tell them of your decision. Your boss is surprised, or mortified, or hurt, or angry, or all of those things. You're told that you're making a big mistake, that your future in your current firm never looked better, that the company you're going to work for isn't right for you. Your boss asks you to give it a few days.

The next day, your boss calls you in to tell you that the company wants to give you a raise, or a promotion, or maybe the assistant you've been asking for but not getting for the past year.

It happens all the time, and the harder your company tries to lure you back, the tougher it sometimes is to decide between going and staying. Let me try to make the decision easier for you. *Go*.

There are exceptions to this advice, to be sure. The offer you get from your current company may, in fact, be so good that you'd be foolish to ignore it, never mind that you've made a commitment somewhere else and never mind that you haven't been happy with your present company for a long time. But the counter offer had better put you into a position of power. If it doesn't, the chances are you're going to be looking for a new job within a year after you accept the counter offer.

I have no hard data to back up this view, only personal experience. In most of the situations I've observed, a person who gives notice and then accepts a counter offer to come back with his or her original firm is generally no longer with that firm after a year (particularly if the counter offer simply sweetens the pie in the existing job). And why should it be otherwise? If you were looking for a new job in the first place, you were probably dissatisfied with more than one aspect of the job, and it's unlikely that the counter offer will get to the root of that dissatisfaction.

In some cases, in fact, the counter offer could worsen these problems. Let's say that a prime source of dissatisfaction is friction between you and your boss. Uneasy with the prospect of losing you, your boss offers a substantial raise. But will the raise ease the friction? Probably not. It will more likely *increase* the friction, because you will now have your boss's resentment to put up with, too.

Trust your earlier instincts. You made a decision to leave your present job because you weren't happy there. You made a decision to accept the job you've been offered because it seems to promise what you've been looking for. Don't disregard the counter offer entirely. Be gracious. Tell your employer how flattered you are. Stay on good terms. But don't let the counter offer blind you to the reality of the situation. If you're swimming across a lake and you're more than halfway across, you don't try to swim back when you start getting tired.

What If You Made a Mistake?

Now let's change the script. You get an offer, accept it, give notice, and start on your new job. Within two months, it hits you: *you made a dumb move*. The company you joined is nothing like you expected. Your job has turned out to be boring and demeaning. Even the added money isn't worth it. You'd do anything to be back in your last job. If you had it to do all over again, you'd never have left.

The best thing to do in this situation is to go back to your original company and see if you can get your old job back again. You heard me. It's not a defeat (not under the present circumstances). It's the most intelligent way to get out of a bad situation. Chances are, if you were good at your job and you left on pleasant terms with everybody, your company will be happy to accept you back. (Then again, your employer may be one of those companies that never forgives an employee for leaving, in which case your chances of coming back are slim.)

It's possible they haven't found your replacement yet. Or maybe your replacement isn't working out. The point is, in this particular situation, your former company is your best shot, so take it. Call up your old boss. Suggest that the two of you get together for lunch or for drinks. You never know: the boss may bring up the matter and tell you how much everybody wishes you were back.

Of course, if you do go back, try to arrange things so that you're not going to be itching to move again in a few months. The two- or three-month separation should be just enough to allow you and your old boss to develop some ideas on how you might get more from the job and give more to the company. Don't worry so much about money (unless money was a big problem in your last job). Concentrate on the day-to-day aspects of the job itself. You may be putting on an old pair of shoes, but it's still important to get off on the right foot.

Handling Your New Job

How to Get Noticed

Naturally, you want to be focusing your energy on the job you've taken, and, naturally, you want to be thinking about advancement within the company. But don't ignore—as too many executives do—the "externals": the things you can do to make yourself attractive to outsiders, to other firms, to head hunters, to recruiters. Here are five points to keep in mind and follow up on:

1. *Be your own PR consultant*. One of the easiest ways is to write articles for trade journals. (You'd be surprised at how easy it is to get published in a trade journal. Most have very small editorial budgets, and are delighted to receive any article that is in any way publishable.) Once you get a few articles published, you'll find that reporters working for the trade journals will seek you out for comments. Be cooperative. As long as you're not compromising privileged company information, nobody is going to mind. Still another way of generating your PR is to write letters to the editors of various papers. Finally, assuming you are at an executive level, make sure that your local paper, if you live in a suburban area, knows that you've been hired for a new job, and has a photograph to run.

2. *Be a joiner*. In case you weren't before, remember? Get active in trade and social organizations. You don't have to go to all the meetings, but make sure you get around enough so that you know what's going on. Keep informed. Stay on top of things.

3. *Try to get listed*. If it's possible and with your boss's permission, see if you can get your name listed under your company's name in major directories like *D & B, Standard & Poor*, and so on.

4. *Become an authority*. You become an authority by becoming a specialist. If you're a CPA, for instance, get on a committee, like a tax committee for your local community. If you have another specialty, offer to give a course in it at your neighborhood school or Y. (Incidentally, you'll be amazed at how much more you yourself will learn about your specialty once you start to teach it.)

Keeping Your Own Personnel File

While you're maintaining this high profile, make sure you keep an open and active file: think of it as your contingency file. Into this file should go names and addresses of contacts, tear sheets or copies of any articles you may have written or any published letters of yours, and any memos or letters written to you that indicate some accomplishment of yours.

Update the file every month. Set aside a half hour or so and make your own contribution to it—a page or two that lists and describes what you accomplished that month on your job. If you keep this up to date and remember to maintain a running account of your accomplishments, you will be that much further ahead of the game the next time you launch a job search (whether because you want to or because you have to). In any case, even if you never have to use the file for finding a new job, it will help you when the time comes to talk about a raise or a promotion. And in the event you want to change jobs, getting a résumé together will be all the easier.

If Things Just Don't Work Out

How to Deal with Being Fired

By now, you should have a good idea of how to get hired, and how to negotiate a good arrangement. Now let's turn to a different problem: getting fired.

Getting fired is one of the most depressing things that can happen to anybody. I know because it's happened to me and to most of the people I know. I don't care how strong your ego is or how much you hated your job, the idea that somebody has decided to get rid of you is a tough pill to swallow. Anybody who says to you, shortly after they've been sacked, "You know something? I'm really glad it happened," is probably lying.

The advice offered most frequently to a person who has just been fired is not to panic. It's not the end of the world, you're told. Most people, at one time or another in their careers, have been fired—even the most successful people. Just look, you're told, at all the successful people who wouldn't be where they are today if, at some point in their career, they weren't bumped from a job they wouldn't otherwise have left.

Okay, it's easy enough for someone who's working to give this advice to someone who's just been tossed out into the cold. As the French writer La Rochefoucauld once said: "We all have strength enough to endure the troubles of others." But the fact of the matter is that, as hard as it may be to accept at the time, getting fired really *isn't* a cause for panic (for concern, yes, but not panic). It really *isn't* the end of the world, and it has indeed happened to most successful people. And while getting fired may not be exactly the "exciting opportunity to grow" some job book authors describe it as, it can be looked upon as a challenge. I could introduce you to dozens and dozens of people (myself included) who wouldn't be where they are today had they not been fired at one time or another in their careers.

I bring up the subject of getting fired here for a couple of reasons. First of all, if you are looking for work while you still have a job you are in a "high risk" category for getting fired. Getting found out, if it happens, is pretty much synonymous with getting fired.

More important, though, is that what you do as an immediate response to getting fired has a strong bearing on the job search that follows. Your response can set you back several weeks, even months. Or it can give you a foundation that will enhance your chances of finding a good—even better—job fairly quickly.

Knowing When It's Coming

Probably the first thing to be said about getting fired is to do everything you possibly can to keep it from happening. True, in some situations, there's nothing you can do. Company revenues drop. An expected project doesn't materialize. An edict comes down from the top to eliminate jobs, and you get the ax. You're not fired, but the job is.

In most situations, however, you get fired because of *you:* because you didn't do your job well enough or because you didn't get along well enough with your superiors.

Whatever the reasons, you can usually sense ahead of time when your job is in jeopardy. You can, that is, if you're alert to the warning signs. Here are some of the more common signs (I call them "fire alarms") that could well mean you're on the firing line:

1. For no apparent reason, your desk is unusually clear and you find you're being given little, if any, new work to do.
2. Several of your subordinates have been promoted to positions above you while you have stayed in one place.
3. The flow of interoffice memos being sent to your attention has slowed to a trickle.
4. Choice assignments that used to go to you routinely are now going to somebody else.
5. Your firm has been acquired by a larger company, raising the possibility that someone from the other company will wind up at your desk.
6. A "consultant," brought in to study your job, asks you surprisingly detailed questions about what you do and how you do it. (It may be that your company wants to "streamline your function." It could also be that the overly inquisitive consultant is gathering information to be passed on to your replacement.)

7. Your company is forced to institute an across-the-board pay cut, and you get a bigger-than-average slice taken out of your paycheck.
8. You are singled out, for no apparent reason, to take a psychological aptitude test.
9. Your boss's attitude toward you changes very noticeably. You find that he (or she) is either much more critical than usual or much less critical than usual.
10. You get moved to a smaller office.
11. You're told you must now share your office with somebody else.

The fact that one or two of these "fire alarms" may be ringing in your job situation should concern but not necessarily alarm you. A cluster of these alarms, however, is a different story. It means you're in deep trouble, and it's time to take some action.

Putting Up a Fight

Being on the firing line doesn't have to mean losing your job. If the situation isn't yet lost—that is, if your replacement hasn't already been hired—you always have a chance to salvage the job, even if it's an outside chance. But you have to do more than simply confront your superiors. You have to be prepared to make changes that will, in turn, change the minds of the people looking to fire you.

The one thing you have going for you, regardless of how tricky the situation may be, is that firing an employee is a messy business that nobody really relishes. Firing you is going to cost your company money. It is going to create transition problems. Besides, nobody really likes to fire anybody. Well, almost nobody. I've met a few hatchet men who seem to take a sadistic pleasure in giving subordinates the ax, but these people represent a tiny minority in the business community. I once had a job years ago in which I had to fire a number of employees at different times. I never got used to it, in fact, I developed a migraine headache every time.

Most executives I know will bend over backwards before firing even the most blatantly incompetent employee. As one personnel director often says: "What amazes me isn't how many people get fired in our company, but how *few* people who really deserve it do get fired."

So, regardless of how dire your situation is, if you can give your superior a reason for *not* firing you, you stand a good chance of avoiding the ax. Remember, though, it may not be easy.

Ask Yourself Some Tough Questions

If your job is in jeopardy, it's your fault. Even if it *isn't* your fault, it's your fault. The superior who has the power to fire you is like the proverbial customer: he or she is always right.

Most people who suspect their jobs are in jeopardy start out by thinking how good a job they've been doing and how big a mistake the company is making in considering dismissal. Spouses or close friends frequently become allies in this pointless exercise. It's just a case of the big, blind, bureaucratic organization not recognizing what a treasure—you—it has in its midst.

Don't make this mistake. As hard as it may be, play devil's advocate with yourself. Don't think about how good you are at your job. Think about any or all of the things you could be doing *wrong*. Ask yourself the following questions:

1. Have you been working as hard or as energetically as you are capable of working and have worked in the past?
2. Are you as enthusiastic about your job as you once were? (Truism: Job performance invariably suffers when enthusiasm dims.)
3. Have you been careless about your appearance (put on a lot of weight, for instance) or about the courtesy you show your fellow workers?
4. Have you allowed personal problems in your life to affect the attention you're giving to your job or the way

you're interacting with your fellow workers? (In other words, are you breaking my law, which states that it's better to take your job problems home with you than it is to take your home problems to the job.)

5. Have you been procrastinating more frequently than you usually do—avoiding decisions?

Put yourself in the position of your boss when you answer these questions. See yourself as your boss sees you. Keep in mind that what you do on the job reflects on your boss. As someone once noted, doing a good job is making your boss look good. Be super-critical of yourself.

If this little experiment doesn't alert you to possible grounds for dismissal, you have a problem. You'd better find suitable grounds, the better to address yourself to them. If it is indeed true that you've been slacking off, that your enthusiasm has been waning, that you've been sloppy about your appearance and your work habits, or that you've been allowing your personal problems to interfere with your job performance, don't waste time looking for excuses. Decide upon some immediate steps to reverse the pattern.

The question now is whether you go to your boss, plead your sins, and make known your intention to mend your ways, or put your new plan into action without letting on that you're doing this out of the fear of getting fired.

There are pros and cons to each strategy. Going to your boss could well be the opportunity your boss has been looking for to tell you the bad news. Thus it could simply hasten your departure. On the other hand, by the time your boss realizes that you've reformed, it may be too late.

A good middle-ground strategy is to set up a meeting with your boss—perhaps a lunch—not to determine whether your job is in jeopardy, but to let the boss know that you yourself are aware that you haven't "been yourself" of late but that the situation is now under control. But it is important that you give the impression you think your job is secure.

Be careful in this session not to go overboard in self-condemnation. Be vague. Don't confess to "sins" you haven't committed, and don't mention anything your boss may not be aware of. Brush over the negatives as quickly as you can. Concentrate on the positives you expect to be present in your job performance before too long.

Another recommended strategy in this situation is to go out of your way to increase your importance to your company. Increase your productivity. Look for extra assignments that demonstrate how interested you are in your job and your company, and show how capable you are as well. Pay special attention to the areas you may be weak in. If you've been short-tempered with your fellow workers, be more polite. If you've been dressing carelessly, spend a few minutes extra every morning making sure you look your best. Remember the basic strategy: Give your would-be firers reasons for *not* firing you.

When the Ax Falls

It may not work, this campaign of yours. So you must prepare yourself for this possibility regardless of how hard you're trying to prevent it from happening. You fight for the job, but you get yourself ready in the event you lose the fight. The bad news, when it comes, will be painful, but it doesn't have to immobilize you. You need to take the news in stride. You will need your wits about you to set up favorable separation arrangements.

Let's set the depressing stage. Your boss has just informed you, presumably with difficulty, that you're going to have to be let go. Maybe you're sitting in the boss's office; maybe the two of you are at lunch. In all likelihood, the boss is going to be kind when you're given this news. You'll be complimented on those aspects of your job performance that were praiseworthy. You'll be told, most likely, that with your skills and personality, you're probably going to be happier and do better somewhere else. You will also be told that the boss and company will do their best to see to it that you find another job without creating too major a disruption in your life.

Let the person firing you deliver the message and, as hard as it may be for you, *don't respond emotionally.* In the event you feel yourself losing control, ask if you can have some time to yourself to collect your thoughts, but do this as a last resort. Go outside and take a walk. Go to a restroom. If you have the urge to cry, do so—get it out of your system. But keep your personal emotional response to yourself. Making your boss feel any worse or more guilty than he or she may already feel isn't going to help your cause one iota. If anything, it's going to make your boss more resentful, more certain you deserved what you got.

Ridiculous though it may seem, the first thing you should be thinking about when you get the bad news is the emotional state of the person giving that news. Forget about yourself for the moment. The situation is almost as painful for the other person as it is for you.

Thank—yes, thank—the person for showing you the consideration of telling you face to face. Thank him or her for the nice things said about you. You might even express some sympathy. Let the other person know that you know how difficult it must be to tell somebody they're fired.

Next, see if you can determine if the situation is totally lost. Don't come right out and ask just how "final" the decision is. That's inviting a final answer, and gets the person off the hook. Make a counter offer. Suggest additional time—a "trial" period of maybe a month.

Watch for the reaction. If the person hedges, mount a counterattack (and if you've anticipated this moment, you should know what to say). Skip the personal sympathy—how badly you need the money now, etc.—and stay with the things that concern your boss, you, and the job. Was your boss aware, for instance, that you've started a particular project a couple of days ago or else cleared up a messy situation that's been hanging on for weeks?

Stick to the concrete. Avoid statments that directly contradict what your boss has said. Even if you consider the criticism unwarranted, grant your boss the possibility that it *is* warranted, but see if you can give some information that may cast you in a different light. Accept blame. If your reports have been coming in consistently late, don't blame your secretary or people in other departments. Acknowledge the problem and state what you intend to do—or better, have already done—to rectify it. "You're right," you might say. "My reports have been late, and I had a meeting two days ago with some of the sales guys so that we can coordinate things better."

Do not, under any circumstances, question the judgment of your boss. Assume that the decision he or she has made has been made with great difficulty, and respect that. The issue isn't whether or not your boss is justified in firing you—that determination has already been made. The question is whether information your boss may not be aware of could induce him or her to reevaluate that decison. At this stage that's all you're looking for, really. A reevaluation, not necessarily a reversal. Play for a draw: additional time. You could use the time either to reclaim your job or to get started on your job search.

Accepting the Inevitable

You should be able to tell by how responsive your boss is to your arguments whether you're getting anywhere or wasting your breath. If the decision seems irrevocable, stop fighting for your job and start negotiating for the most favorable separation conditions possible. Be hard-nosed with yourself. There comes a point in these discussions when the more you resist, the harder it will be for you to negotiate for severance concessions from the company.

Your company has a policy for dismissed employees. Know what it is *before* you get fired. Your boss has some flexibility, but can only deviate so far from company policy. You're not going to get the moon unless it's in your contract, so don't bother to ask for it. Make requests, not demands. You'll get more.

You'll probably discuss severance arrangements with the person who fires you, which is good and bad. The good part is that many executives, to ease the guilt that comes with firing somebody, are unduly generous when it comes to severance benefits. The bad part is that your negotiating power is limited somewhat by your need to get a favorable reference from your boss.

Money, of course, is not the only issue in severance negotiations. You'll want the maximum amount the company is willing to pay, but don't overlook other benefits that may be just as important. See if you can have an office and secretarial services throughout the course of your campaign. If you've had access to a company car as part of your position, see if you can maintain the use of the car for several more weeks. Your company may have an outplacement service—more and more companies are setting them up. Take advantage of it, or ask for the money the company would spend on outplacement in the form of severance. Don't allow wounded pride to deny you anything your company is willing to give in order to help you find a new job.

A final piece of advice about being fired. After the smoke has cleared, either write your boss or arrange for a meeting whose purpose is to find out where you went wrong. (A letter may be better since your boss may be reluctant to level with you in a direct meeting.) Stress the fact that you want honest answers, no matter how critical those answers are. And when you get this information, *learn from it*. If you can learn something about yourself from being fired—something that may help you become successful in your next job—then the experience will have had some benefit for you.

Don't waste this opportunity for growth. Otherwise, you may find yourself in the same position three or four months after you start your next job.

Conclusion

Now that you've finished this book, you have a choice to make. You can incorporate into your job-search strategy the ideas and suggestions I've been giving you throughout this book, or you can follow the same "hit or miss" pattern you may have been following *before* you read this book. The choice may seem easy on the surface, yet I've found that many job-hunters, for reasons I've never understood, ignore the fundamentals of job searching even though they recognize the importance and value of these fundamentals.

I hope you're different. As I said early on in this book, job-hunting is one tough job, and I would be the last person to tell you that following the advice I've given you is the easiest route to go when you're looking for a job. But I *know* the techniques described in this book work. I know because I have seen them work time and time again over the past thirty years. And they can work for you—providing, that is, you put them into practice. So, go to it. Never forget that there are very few things in life as important as having a job that's right for you. And keep in mind that all the work you put into getting hired for this job is going to pay you dividends for a long time to come. Good luck!

All people are, in one
way or another, imperfect.
But imperfect people look
to hire perfect people.

WHAT THE SURVEYS SHOWED

As part of the research for this book, I hired a leading firm, Burke Marketing Research, Inc., to conduct two surveys: one among personnel executives, the other among top management. Here is a summary of the key findings.

The *majority* of top management executives agree that:

1. Personality and intelligence, in most cases can compensate for a lack of specific job experience.

2. In general, demonstrating aggressiveness and assertiveness in the job interview will enhance your chances of being hired.

3. Most interviewers will take notice of whether or not you look them in the eye.

4. Having been fired from your previous job will *not* necessarily prevent you from being hired, everything else being equal.

5. Being divorced is *not* a handicap in most hiring situations.

6. Basic enthusiasm is one of the most important qualifications for most jobs.

7. Showing up late for an interview *will* hurt your chances of being hired.

8. Virtually all unsolicited letters written to top executives get read and most draw some response.

The majority of personnel managers believe that:

1. Wearing jeans to an interview (regardless of your sex) will hurt your chances of being hired.

2. Being overweight is a definite disadvantage when you're looking for a job.

3. How you dress is a very important consideration to most interviewers.

4. Your interviewer will be able to tell when you are exaggerating your skills.

5. Your chances of being hired are better if you appear to be overconfident than they would be if you appeared to be shy.

6. Most interviewers are more interested in you as a person than in your specific skills and background.

7. Not knowing anything about the company interviewing you will hurt your chances of being hired.

THE INFLUENTIAL FACTOR SCALE

Burke researchers asked personnel executives to name the most influential factors in their decision. Here is how the list turned out in order of their importance:

1. Your personality: how you present yourself during the interview.

2. Your experience.

3. The qualifications you show for the job you're being interviewed for.

4. Your background and references.

5. The enthusiasm you show toward the company and the job.

6. Your educational and technical background.

7. Your growth potential.

8. Your compatibility (i.e. ability to get along with co-workers).

9. Your intelligence and capacity to learn.

10. How hard a worker you appear to be.

Application
For Employment

(PLEASE PRINT)

> Qualified applicants are considered for all positions without regard to race. color, religion, sex, national origin, age, marital or veteran status, or the presence of a non-job-related medical condition or handicap.

Date of Application _____

Position(s) Applied For _____

Referral Source: ☐ Advertisement   ☐ Friend   ☐ Relative

☐ Employment Agency   ☐ Other

Name _____
       LAST   FIRST   MIDDLE

Address _____
         NUMBER   STREET   CITY   STATE   ZIP CODE

Phone No. (_____) _____ Social Security No. _____
           AREA CODE

Have you filed an application here before?   ☐ Yes   ☐ No   Date _____

Have you ever been employed here before?   ☐ Yes   ☐ No   Date _____

Are you a citizen of the United States?   ☐ Yes   ☐ No

If not, do you possess an Alien Registration Card?   ☐ Yes   ☐ No

If yes, give Alien Registration Number _____

Are you available to work?   ☐ Full Time   ☐ Part Time   ☐ Shift Work

Are you on lay-off and subject to recall?   ☐ Yes   ☐ No

Can you travel if a job requires it?   ☐ Yes   ☐ No

Do any of your friends or relatives, other than your spouse, work here?   ☐ Yes   ☐ No

If yes, list name(s) _____

Have you been convicted of a felony within the last 7 years?   ☐ No   ☐ Yes

If yes, explain _____
_____
_____

AN EQUAL EMPLOYMENT OPPORTUNITY EMPLOYER M/F/V/H

Are you a veteran of the U.S. military service?　☐ Yes　☐ No

If yes, what was your Branch of U.S. military service? _____

Do you have any physical, mental or medical impairment
or disability that would limit your job performance
for the position for which you are applying?　　　☐ Yes　　☐ No

If yes, please explain _____

What foreign languages do you speak, read and/or write?

	FLUENTLY	GOOD	FAIR
SPEAK			
READ			
WRITE			

List professional, trade, business or civic activities and offices held. (Exclude groups which indicate race, color, religion, sex or national origin):

_____
_____
_____

Give name, address and phone number of three references not related to you.

_____
_____
_____

Special Employment Notice To Disabled Veterans, Vietnam Era Veterans, And Individuals With Physical Or Mental Handicaps

Government contractors are subject to Section 402 of the Vietnam Era Veterans Readjustment Act of 1974 which requires that they take affirmative action to employ and advance in employment qualified disabled veterans and veterans of the Vietnam Era, and Section 503 of the Rehabilitation Act of 1973, as amended, which requires government contractors to take affirmative action to employ and advance in employment qualified handicapped individuals.

If you are a disabled veteran, or have a physical or mental handicap, you are invited to volunteer this information. The purpose is to provide information regarding proper placement and appropriate accommodation to enable you to perform the job in a proper and safe manner. This information will be treated as confidential. Failure to provide this information will not jeopardize or adversely affect any consideration you may receive for employment.

If you wish to be identified, please sign below.

☐ Handicapped Individual　　☐ Disabled Veteran　　☐ Vietnam Era Veteran

Signed _____

Employment Experience

List each job held. Start with your Present or Last job. Include military service assignments and volunteer activities. (Exclude groups which indicate race, color, religion, sex or national origin.)

		Dates		Work Performed
1	Employer	From	To	Work Performed
	Address			
	Job Title	Hrly. Rate/Salary		
		Starting	Final	
	Supervisor			
	Reason for Leaving			
2	Employer	Dates		Work Performed
		From	To	
	Address			
	Job Title	Hrly. Rate/Salary		
		Starting	Final	
	Supervisor			
	Reason for Leaving			
3	Employer	Dates		Work Performed
		From	To	
	Address			
	Job Title	Hrly. Rate/Salary		
		Starting	Final	
	Supervisor			
	Reason for Leaving			
4	Employer	Dates		Work Performed
		From	To	
	Address			
	Job Title	Hrly. Rate/Salary		
		Starting	Final	
	Supervisor			
	Reason for Leaving			

If you need additional space, please continue on a separate sheet of paper.

Summarize Special Skills and Qualifications
Acquired From Employment Or Other Experience _____

_____

_____

_____

_____

Education

	Elementary				High				College/University				Graduate/Professional			
School Name																
Years Completed:(Circle)	4	5	6	7	8	9	10	11	12	1	2	3	4	1	2	3	4
Diploma/Degree																
Describe Course Of Study:																
Describe Specialized Training, Apprenticeship, Skills, and Extra-Curricular Activities																

Honors Received:

State any additional information you feel may be helpful to us in considering your application.

Agreement

I certify that answers given herein are true and complete to the best of my knowledge.

I authorize investigation of all statements contained in this application for employment as may be necessary in arriving at an employment decision.

In the event of employment, I understand that false or misleading information given in my application or interview(s) may result in discharge. I understand, also, that I am required to abide by all rules and regulations of the Company.

Signature of Applicant   Date

For Personnel Department Use Only

Arrange Interview   ☐ Yes   ☐ No

Remarks _____

_____
                                              INTERVIEWER   DATE

Employed   ☐ Yes   ☐ No   Date of Employment _____

Job Title _____ Hourly Rate/Salary _____ Department _____

          By _____
                              NAME/TITLE   DATE

Applicant Data Record

(PLEASE PRINT)

Qualified applicants are considered for all positions, and employees are treated during employment without regard to race, color, religion, sex, national origin, age, marital or veteran status, medical condition or handicap.

As employers/government contractors, we comply with government regulations and affirmative action responsibilities.

Solely, to help us comply with government record keeping, reporting and other legal requirements, please fill out the Data Record.

This Data is for periodic government reporting and will be kept in a <u>Confidential File</u> separate from the Application for Employment.

Date _____

Position(s) Applied For _____

Referral Source: ☐ Advertisement ☐ Friend ☐ Relative
☐ Employment Agency ☐ Other _____

Name _____ Phone (___)
LAST FIRST MIDDLE AREA CODE

Address _____
NUMBER STREET CITY STATE ZIP CODE

DETACH HERE

Affirmative Action Survey

Government agencies require periodic reports on the sex, ethnicity, handicapped and veteran status of applicants. This data is for analysis and affirmative action only. Submission of information about a handicap is voluntary.

Check one:
☐ Male ☐ Female

Check one of the following:
Race/Ethnic Group: ☐ White ☐ Black ☐ Hispanic
☐ American Indian/Alaskan Native ☐ Asian/Pacific Islander

Check if any of the following are applicable:
☐ Vietnam Era Veteran ☐ Disabled Veteran ☐ Handicapped Individual

Re-order Form #25960 From Amsterdam Printing and Litho Corp., Amsterdam, N.Y. 12010
© copyright 1980 Amsterdam Printing and Litho Corp., Amsterdam, N.Y. 12010

FOR PERSONNEL DEPARTMENT USE ONLY		
Position(s) Applied For Is Open: ☐ Yes ☐ No		
Position(s) Considered For: _____		
_____		
Date _____		

NOTES:

DETACH HERE

EMPLOYMENT INTERVIEW REPORT

TO: _____

FROM: _____

NAME OF APPLICANT: _____

ADDRESS _____ PHONE _____

CANDIDATE _____ (Job Title)

DATE OF THIS INTERVIEW: _____

THIS IS: 1st INTERVIEW ☐ 2nd INTERVIEW ☐ 3rd INTERVIEW ☐

INTERVIEWER: _____

PLEASE REPORT YOUR INTERVIEW IMPRESSIONS BY CHECKING THE ONE MOST APPROPRIATE BOX IN EACH AREA.

1. APPEARANCE (If relevant to the particular job.)			
☐ Very untidy, poor taste in dress.	☐ Somewhat careless about personal appearance.	☐ Satisfactory personal appearance.	☐ Good taste in dress; better than average appearance.	☐ Unusually well groomed; very neat; excellent taste in dress.

2. FRIENDLINESS (If relevant to the particular job.)			
☐ Appears very distant and aloof.	☐ Approachable; fairly friendly.	☐ Warm, friendly, sociable.	☐ Very sociable and outgoing.	☐ Extremely friendly and sociable.

3. POISE-STABILITY			
☐ Ill at ease; is "jumpy" and appears nervous.	☐ Somewhat tense; is easily irritated.	☐ About as poised as the average applicant.	☐ Confident; appears to like crises more than average person.	☐ Extremely well composed; apparently thrives under pressure.

213

4. PERSONALITY (an individual's behavior characteristics or personal suitability for the job)

	☐	☐	☐	☐	☐
4. PERSONALITY	Unsatisfactory for this job.	Questionable for this job.	Satisfactory for this job.	Very desirable for this job.	Outstanding for this job.
5. CONVERSATIONAL ABILITY	Talks very little; expression poor.	Attempts expression but does fair job at best.	Average fluency and expression.	Talks well and "to the point."	Excellent expression; extremely fluent; forceful.
6. ALERTNESS	Slow to "catch on."	Rather slow; requires more than average explanation.	Grasps ideas with average ability.	Quick to understand; perceives very well.	Exceptionally keen and alert.
7. INFORMATION ABOUT GENERAL WORK FIELD	Poor knowledge of field.	Fair knowledge of field.	Is as informed as the average applicant.	Fairly well informed; knows more than average applicant.	Has excellent knowledge of the field.
8. EXPERIENCE	No relationship between applicant's background and job requirements.	Fair relationship between applicant's background and job requirement.	Average amount of meaningful background and experience.	Background very good; considerable experience.	Excellent background and experience.
9. DRIVE	Has poorly defined goals and appears to set without purpose.	Appears to set goals too low and to put forth little effort to achieve these.	Appears to have average goals; puts forth average effort to reach these.	Appears to strive hard; has high desire to achieve.	Appears to set high goals and to strive incessantly to achieve more.
10. OVERALL	Definitely unsatisfactory.	Substandard.	Average.	Definitely above average.	Outstanding.

© Copyright 1963, 1978—V.W. EIMICKE ASSOCIATES, INC., Bronxville, N.Y. Printed in U.S.A.
Form 103

(PLEASE SEE REVERSE SIDE)

214

THIS APPLICANT SHOULD BE HIRED: YES ☐   NO ☐ IF NO, STATE REASON: _____

_____

_____

_____

IF NO, WOULD YOU RECOMMEND CONSIDERATION AT FUTURE DATE FOR THIS OR ANY OTHER POSITION?

YES ☐   NO ☐   REMARKS _____

_____

_____

_____

TYPE OF WORK FOR WHICH APPLICANT APPEARS BEST QUALIFIED: _____

_____

_____

_____

ADDITIONAL COMMENTS: _____

TELEPHONE PRE-EMPLOYMENT REFERENCE CHECK GUIDE

APPLICANT _____ Name _____ Soc. Sec. Number _____

CANDIDATE FOR _____ Job Title _____

DATE OF
REF. CHECK _____ CHECKED BY _____

PREVIOUS
EMPLOYER
{ COMPANY NAME _____

ADDRESS _____ No. _____ Street _____ City _____ State _____ Telephone _____

PERSON
TALKED TO _____ Name _____ Title _____

INTRODUCE YOURSELF BY NAME, TITLE AND COMPANY

(Name of applicant) has applied for employment with us and has told us that he/she previously worked for your Organization. I should like to verify some information given us. Do you have time to answer a few questions? (If not, get a definite time to recall.)

1. Was applicant employed by your Organization?   YES _____   NO _____→

2. Applicant states that employment was from _____ to _____
   Is that correct? YES _____ NO _____. If not, show correct dates: from _____ to _____

3. What was applicant's job when starting to work for you? _____

4. What was applicant's job when leaving? _____

5. Applicant states earnings of $ _____ per _____ Is that correct? YES _____ NO _____
   If not, show actual rate $ _____ per _____

6. What did you think of the quality of applicant's work? _____

_____

_____

_____

(PLEASE SEE REVERSE SIDE)

7. How hard did applicant work? _____

8. Was applicant regular and punctual in attendance? YES_____ NO_____

   Did applicant lose any time because of poor health? YES_____ NO_____

   If yes, explain: _____
   _____

9. How did applicant get along with others? _____
   _____

10. Did applicant follow instructions? YES_____ NO_____

11. Did applicant have any domestic or personal trouble which

    interfered with work? YES_____ NO_____ Any financial difficulties? YES_____ NO

    Any drinking or gambling problems? YES_____ NO_____

    If yes, explain: _____
    _____
    _____
    _____

12. Why did applicant leave your Organization? _____

_____

_____

_____

13. Would you re-employ? YES_____ NO_____ If not, why not? _____

_____

14. In summing up, what would you say are applicant's strong points? _____

_____

Weak points? _____

_____

Additional information _____

_____

_____

_____

PRE-EMPLOYMENT REFERENCE CHECK

_____ 19 ___

Attention: _____

Gentlemen:

The applicant named below has told us that he/she previously worked for your Company. We would appreciate your furnishing us with as much of the information requested below as possible. We assure you that any information you may give will be treated confidentially.

An early reply will be greatly appreciated.

Sincerely yours,

_____ _____
                                                    Title

Co. Name: _____

Co. Address: _____

APPLICANT'S NAME _____ SOCIAL SECURITY NUMBER _____

DATES IN YOUR EMPLOY: FROM _____ TO _____ SALARY: $ _____ PER _____

POSITION HELD _____

Is the information listed above correct? YES _____ NO _____ If no, please supply the correct information below.

_____

Why did applicant leave your Company? _____

Would you re-employ? YES _____ NO _____ If no, why not? _____

_____

Please rate applicant on the following characteristics:

	POOR	FAIR	AVERAGE	VERY GOOD	EXCELLENT
QUALITY OF WORK					
QUANTITY OF WORK					
SUITABILITY FOR POSITION					
* PERSONAL APPEARANCE					
ATTENDANCE					
DEPENDABILITY					
COOPERATIVENESS					
CREATIVENESS					

* If relevant to the particular job.

DATE _____   SIGNED _____

                                     TITLE _____

INDEX